MY BLACK MOTHERHOOD

of related interest

Overcoming Everyday Racism
Building Resilience and Wellbeing in the Face
of Discrimination and Microaggressions
Susan Cousins
ISBN 978 1 78592 850 5
eISBN 978 1 78592 851 2

Postnatal PTSD
A Guide for Health Professionals
Kim Thomas with Shona McCann
ISBN 978 1 78775 620 5
eISBN 978 1 78775 621 2

Surviving Post-Natal Depression
At Home, No One Hears You Scream
Cara Aiken
ISBN 978 1 85302 861 8
eISBN 978 1 84642 262 1

Supporting Breastfeeding Past the First Six Months and Beyond
A Guide for Professionals and Parents
Emma Pickett
ISBN 978 1 78775 989 3
eISBN 978 1 78775 990 9

Supporting Queer Birth
A Book for Birth Professionals and Parents
AJ Silver
ISBN 978 1 83997 045 0
eISBN 978 1 83997 046 7

'The transition into motherhood can be difficult for many women, but cultural expectations, socialization, religious beliefs, racism and biases add layer upon layer of additional challenges for Black mothers. Sandra's book is honest and raw, providing an analytical lens by documenting and reflecting on daily lived encounters whilst also asserting the validity of Black mothers' knowledge. A must-read for anyone working in perinatal services who wants to improve their cultural competence and understand their biases.'

– Kicki Hansard, doula and author of Secrets of Birth

'Sandra's book gives a wonderfully candid insight into the experiences and obstacles faced by Black mums all over the country. It's one that ALL health professionals need to have on their bookshelves.'

– Marley Hall, midwife, speaker and content creator,
www.midwifemarley.com

'As a Black mum in Britain, I've experienced some of the pressures and challenges that Sandra Igwe explores in her book – from a difficult birth to feeling isolated and misunderstood by health practitioners. In *My Black Motherhood*, Sandra shares deeply affecting stories of Black maternity and mental health and lays out a pathway for change, starting by challenging narratives like the 'Strong Black Woman' trope. Reading Sandra's book is like listening to a passionate, relatable sister-friend who will help you fight your corner or offer you a shoulder to cry on if you need it. *My Black Motherhood* acts as both a powerful call to action and a safe space for Black mums to feel seen and heard at last. I'm so grateful to Sandra for raising her voice and for stirring up "good trouble" on this vital cause.'

– Uju Asika, author of Bringing Up Race: How to Raise
a Kind Child in a Prejudiced World

'*My Black Motherhood* is an eye-opening read that gives a platform to often unheard voices. Sandra Igwe does a brilliant job of not only highlighting the myriad challenges Black mothers are up against, but also championing tangible solutions. Regardless of your connection to the topic, everyone has something to learn from this book.'

– Jess Austin, First-Person and Opinion Editor, Metro.co.uk

'I found the book incredibly powerful. Sandra has captured not only her own experiences but those of many other Black mothers – using her own words it is an excellent "jumping-off point to investigate your own prejudices". It made me recognize how little I know and understand of (again using Sandra's words) "multidimensional, multifaceted and multi-layered" Black motherhood. I started my reading thinking I would highlight some key quotes to share with others but ended up highlighting one on almost every page. Perhaps the two sentences that stood out most for me were: "Trust is earned" and "Being Black comes with its struggles, being a woman comes with struggles and being a mother comes with its struggles, so imagine being all three". Thank you, Sandra, for the opportunity to read this – it made me laugh, it made me cry, but above all, it made me think and question.'

– Marian Knight, Professor of Maternal and Child Population Health, University of Oxford

My Black Motherhood

Mental Health, Stigma,
Racism and the System

Sandra Igwe

Jessica Kingsley Publishers
London and Philadelphia

First published in Great Britain in 2022 by Jessica Kingsley Publishers
An imprint of Hodder & Stoughton Ltd
An Hachette UK Company

1

A CIP catalogue record for this title is available from the British Library
and the Library of Congress

ISBN 978 1 83997 008 5
eISBN 978 1 83997 009 2

Jessica Kingsley Publishers' policy is to use papers that are natural,
renewable and recyclable products and made from wood grown in
sustainable forests. The logging and manufacturing processes are expected
to conform to the environmental regulations of the country of origin.

Jessica Kingsley Publishers
Carmelite House
50 Victoria Embankment
London EC4Y 0DZ

www.jkp.com

Contents

CHAPTER 1

When Reality Does Not Match Expectations

I sat on the edge of my bed, arms shaking and aching because I had held her for so long. It was almost dark, with just the illuminating night light on, and although I sang her favourite lullaby that somehow made her unwind, my voice could not be heard. I stayed silent on what I had experienced from 3 March 2016: my treatment, the expectations, my perinatal mind, being dismissed. I was unable to hear and be heard by all the other Black mothers who, like me, had embarked on their journey into motherhood. Born and raised in South London, I watched my Nigerian mother do absolutely everything for me and my three sisters. She just did it all: cleaning, cooking, braiding our hair, ironing our uniforms, taking us to church – the list went on. Sometimes I struggle to even remember her just sitting down and resting – I mean, what was rest when there was always something to be done? From the gaze of my young and naive eyes, there was a perception that she always seemed to float through mother-hood like a swan gliding over a still lake. If there was any frantic legwork going on under the water, it was never obvious to me or my sisters.

Motherhood looked easy, effortless, my personal calling, and I looked forward, eagerly, to the day I would be a mother. After all, that was what my mother named me: Sandra 'Nneoma':

Nneoma
Name meaning 'good mother' in the Igbo language, southeastern Nigeria.
Most *Nneomas* are true to their names: they make good mothers. For example, 'My daughter is an *Nneoma*. *Nneoma* will never let her child go hungry.'

Traditional African names often have unique stories and meanings behind them. From the day or time a baby is born to the circumstances surrounding the birth, several factors influence the names parents choose for their children.

So was I destined to be a 'good mother'? Even if the pressure wasn't in my name, so many other popular African phrases and sayings place motherhood at the pinnacle of womanhood. Even the Yoruba adage 'Iya ni wura' means 'mother is gold'. Sheesh, gold! Gold is the best-known precious metal for many reasons, but the most noteworthy is its sturdy links to global economies throughout history. It's been used as currency for hundreds and hundreds of years. And that's exactly what motherhood is within the Black community – arguably the most inherently valuable status and currency.

I remember when people asked me what I wanted to be when I grew up, I would always say that I wanted to be a mum, but my own mum would laugh and say in her Nigerian accent, 'Yes, that will be fine, it will come, but, in the meantime, you need to have a career too!'

Whenever I saw a woman walking down the road pushing a buggy, I would think that this is a person who is the most graceful and beautiful of human beings, who is almost elevated to sainthood just by virtue of the fact that she is a mother. Ironically, looking back now, I can see that this was a very unrealistic and even a toxic view, and maybe that was where the seeds for my own and many other Black women's problems were sown.

My mum wasn't the only woman I looked up to as a child. One of my aunts helped raise us, too. She was a nurse who worked long hours caring for others on a daily basis. She helped my mum and formed part of our immediate community; she even frequently watched us when my mum needed to run errands and often dropped me off to nursery while my mum took my older sister to school. Alongside my mother, my aunt bought us gifts and treats – sweets and new clothes. 'These are my daughters,' she'd say proudly to anyone who came across us. I adored being seen as my aunt's child. I was, wasn't I? She didn't literally give birth to us, but she was every bit as important as my own mum and we had formed that bond that was hard to shake. When she passed away when I was 21, my world came crashing down; I grieved achingly for her as I would any loved parent. My general practitioner (GP) prescribed antidepressants during this period, which I hid under my bed and never actually took. Although I was so desperate for this pain to go away, I could never take medication to help me deal with my emotions, my sadness... I felt weak, ashamed and confused.

I remember my aunt sharing her desires of wanting to be a mother herself, a biological mum, but sadly for her, it never happened. Sometimes, I wonder if she thought that was the only way to live her life to the fullest, to have further purpose or a new meaning. But she had a purpose to me...though I often caught glimpses of her craving and longing for something else.

From an early age, motherhood and a career seemed destined for two different women – two different Sandras. How could I possibly work a full-time demanding job like my aunt and raise children like my mum? There couldn't possibly be enough hours in the day. How could anyone take on so much?

After university, I lived more independently, started my career, travelled and enjoyed the perks of socializing, I began to have doubts and wondered if motherhood was really going to be for me. The idea that another being, my child, would be looking to me for everything seemed frightening. Surely, motherhood would come naturally, wouldn't it? As the umbilical cord was cut, the necessary mechanisms would click into place that would magically equip me for a life as a mother. Until then, however, I felt as though I was fine just concentrating on me and pushed my concerns about how I would cope with a baby and the irrevocability of having another human being to care for to the back of my mind. Meanwhile, however, the pressure was on, and as each year ticked by, my Nigerian aunties would lament:

'Where is your husband, Sandra? Time is getting on, you know!'

'When are you going to get married, where are your babies?'

I was a curiosity: a woman of child-bearing age, approaching my mid-20s, but there was no sign of me following the traditional route of getting married and reproducing.

Then everything changed: I met my husband and I fell pregnant, and no doubt huge sighs of familial relief were expelled. But it seems that being married and pregnant was not enough, because before my first daughter, Zoe, even made an appearance, I was being asked about the next baby, as though there was no question that there would be another child, and another, and another! It seems where Black womanhood is concerned, enough is never enough. There seems to be a timescale. The pressure is on and expectations are sky-high.

What happens to Black women who have children but experience difficulties with motherhood? What happens when reality does not match expectations? The concept of motherhood is invariably portrayed to be a magical, beautiful and powerful role. When I became a mother, and nothing looked as I thought it would, I wanted to access support, but struggled. Instead, I was silent. And at the onset of trying to cry out for help, those who I thought were in a position to assist perpetuated more silence.

Like everyone else, I had been fed the rhetoric that becoming a mother meant I would immediately be elevated to a place where I was selfless, put my child first, always, and attended joyfully to their needs without a single qualm or twinge of discomfort.

> As a Black mother, I felt almost forced to be excited in my pregnancy, and if you don't look extremely happy all the time, family and friends will think there is something wrong with you. Shame literally fills you...

> – Michelle Nwaike

As perfect as my precious Zoe was, the reality of my early days of motherhood was all about sleepless nights, grinding exhaustion, anxiety, stress, feelings of isolation and an overwhelming sense of guilt that I just could not cope. But the hardest part for me was that no one was speaking about this massive elephant in the room. I had to bite my lips, put on my brave face and fix my mask. I had to be seen as a 'good mother' at all costs.

I can see now that my unrealistic expectations of motherhood definitely led to my challenges adjusting to being a mother, and the 'new reality' of my life. They probably also led to the delay in a diagnosis of postnatal depression and anxiety, but they were also the reason why I set up The Motherhood Group shortly after giving birth to Zoe, a social enterprise for the Black maternal experience.

Listening to thousands of Black mothers' stories, highs, lows and challenges through this safe space that I created, essentially for myself at the lowest point of my life, ultimately led to me no longer wanting to be silent.

I will reference many of the experiences shared with me through The Motherhood Group, which started initially as a WhatsApp chat in 2016. Many of the mothers in this chat – myself included – needed support during and after the birth of their children, whether due to medical racism or simple neglect or wanting a community of mothers who just understood.

'I'm so glad I found this chat :),' a new mother typed.

'I don't have many mum friends, and there's not many Black mums in my new area.'

'A nurse told me not to give my baby water until six months, but my Nigerian mum says to do it from birth. What did you all do?'

'How long until you started having sex again?' another asked.

'My breasts are leaking so much! I don't want to leak on my husband. Lol.'

Other mothers wanted to know which traditional customs some of us chose to maintain, and which we left behind. It was almost like a digital tribe, where all the mothers cared for each other and offered support.

I imagine this is what my mum meant when she said that 'it takes a village'.

Generally, Black women are expected, without question, to create, nurture and provide for their progeny without a murmur. There is an absolute belief that this is something that every woman does without any effort, as easily as she breathes in and out. Within this perceived truth is incalculable personal, cultural and social significance. There is no doubt that there will be different influences on navigating motherhood, such as racism, colourism, culture and classism, making a hard job even more difficult.

Or should we acknowledge that for many becoming a mother

is one of the most personal and social confirmations of identity? While giving birth to my daughters, I basically rebirthed a new version of myself; I was a new Sandra. After all, for many Black women, motherhood is a symbol of womanhood. For many, it can provide a courteous social identity, a sense of importance – some would even say access to close resource networks, and a space where authority, a sense of control and self-expression can be cultivated.

I've always suspected that in the past, Black women have defined and experienced motherhood with an attribution of womanhood linked to domesticity, the ability of the woman to take care of her home, strength, leadership and her ability to lead in male absence.

My expectations of Black motherhood may have been the road to empowerment but this was quickly clouded by a plethora of pressures that came with this role:

motherhood as a never-ending source of emotional comfort and support

motherhood as the epitome of strength and self-confidence

motherhood as unconditional endless love.

In Nigeria, traditionally a woman may only consider herself to be a 'real' woman when she has proved that she is fertile and when the halo of maternity is shining over her. This wild idea holds true for many African Black women, for whom being a mother is the definition of being a real woman or at least a 'responsible' woman. This leads to the idea that to be socially acceptable a woman who is married needs also to be a mother, and if this woman does not manage to have a child, she may feel rejected and suffer with feelings of low self-esteem. There are many examples in African literature, such as the character Nnu Ego in Buchi Emecheta's

Joys of Motherhood; sadly, she does not even consider herself to be a woman until she starts having children.[1] I wonder if this was how my aunt felt for many years before she passed away? It honestly breaks my heart if she even felt a fraction of this.

As harmful as this rhetoric is, in many cultures a 'childless woman' will be seen as a 'waste' to her husband and to herself, and despite the fact we are in the 21st century, there are many places where these views of womanhood, and more specifically motherhood, still hold very true. To make matters worse, there are some rituals that take place for child-bearing women that still survive, such as 'stakor' where a portion of a woman's front tooth is chipped off with a hammer so that all the world will see that she is a married woman and a mother. In the places that this happens, it is seen as a badge of honour.

I had to share a bit of context, just so you, the reader, can fully understand the entirety of what 'motherhood' can look like to the Black community. The context I have given naturally comes from my own personal experiences as a woman, growing up in the UK, but with a Nigerian background – specifically Igbo. Of course, it will be extremely difficult to encompass every single Black woman's experience – this will differ by country, tradition, age, faith and family structure – but I truly believe there are similar expectations across many Black communities as a whole which I hope you can find in this book.

When I set out to create a space for Black mothers to communicate and support one another, I had a basic outline of what I hoped to accomplish. I wanted Black women to talk about our particular trials and tribulations, as well as our joys and accomplishments, although not everyone in my life and spectators supported my efforts.

'Aren't you racist for excluding non-Black women?' an acquaintance asked after I spoke to her about my group.

I was shocked; that comment stung – and then I felt anger. As if Black women aren't de facto excluded from white spaces all the f*cking time? I wanted to shout at her, swear and scream. This wasn't rocket science – why didn't she understand? Did I have to explain to her why Black mothers needed a safe space? I couldn't find what I needed in the world. I didn't feel secure around maternity or mental health services, or any 'support' out there, and definitely not around her. That was the last time we spoke properly.

Nobody even wanted to talk to me in the white Mummy and Baby groups – did she call them racist? But *I* was the issue – someone who finally had the courage and strength to create my own form of culturally competent support. The obvious option was to create my own safe space for myself and other Black women. *How is that difficult to understand?*

'You're not going to be able to get possible future funding if you don't include white women,' another friend said. She was like a mentor to me. 'If you want The Motherhood Group to become sustainable one day, you must include white mums – that's where the funding is.'

But I didn't care, I was stubborn because I knew there was a critical need. I was faithful to other Black women; I was true to myself.

Over time, The Motherhood Group developed beyond my initial ideas. It became more powerful and more compassionate than I ever imagined.

At a recent event hosted by The Motherhood Group, I asked the nearly 100 participants what were their 'current fears, challenges and thoughts' at that present moment in time, and asked them to write them down on the tiny pieces of paper on their table, and to put them in the clear jar that we passed around the room.

So many mothers came forward with questions and concerns about the particularities of Black motherhood. You can read some of them below:

> Maintaining good mental health as a single mum with little support nearby. Co-parenting with a toxic baby daddy :/
>
> Is there a limit to how much you can buy your child? Am I wrong for wanting some time out?
>
> Not doing enough. Not enough sleep. Not enough 'going out'.
>
> How can more Black British mums advocate for themselves?
>
> Anyone with imposter syndrome?
>
> Concerned about going into labour after statistics show Black mothers are more likely to die during labour in comparison to other ethnics.
>
> Big age gap with siblings. How do I encourage a healthy relationship?
>
> Feeling confident/better about yourself while in your new body?
>
> Being mindful.
>
> What expectations do you have of Black female professionals e.g. GP, midwives, etc.?
>
> Feeling you're not doing enough.
>
> Soo many ideas, want to be independent and make my own money. However motivation is very low + drive to proceed and start.
>
> Trying to find yourself again after motherhood.
>
> How to find yourself after having a baby? Sense of loss of self.

Disciplining kids w/o hitting. Co-parenting with someone who is not consistent or trustworthy.

How do you deal with your daughter she is sexually active at 17?

How to deal with co-parenting and mum anxiety?

Making time for yourself, self-care.

I have so much to do, not sure how to spend time on all of them.

How do you balance work life, business and motherhood together without feeling less of a mother?

Handling in-law relationships – power struggles, unwanted opinions, negativity.

Losing weight. Still not at my goal weight prior to having a baby.

How to practise and exercise patience with 6-year-old and 4-year-old.

With more than one child, how can we give time and love to each of them and find time for yourself and partner?

Black motherhood & mental health. Not seen as a 'real thing'. It affects us especially badly. Drugs are given too easily. Doctors should be trauma informed.

Meet Katie Bonful, a Black mum to one who also saw motherhood as a badge of honour. I met her through The Motherhood Group and was blown away by her personal story and experience. She also spoke at our event, which left everyone in the room in tears.

In African culture it's often seen as a woman's right to bear a child. As soon as you get married the questions follow as to when you will have a child, and this pressure can be so overwhelming. When you finally discover that you are pregnant, there is so much noise and jubilation.

However, what if you suffer a loss through miscarriage or still-birth? It is the total opposite. There is so much silence.

Over the course of an 18-month period, I had experienced two consecutive second-trimester miscarriages. And they both occurred on the same day a year apart. As a Black woman, my knowledge of baby loss was very little until I went through it myself.

I lost my first baby, a boy on 9th March 2017, and exactly a year later on 9th March 2018 I also lost another boy. Both pregnancies ended when I was 17 weeks pregnant. Both pregnancies also ended at the same hospital, I was in the same hospital room as the year before where I had to go through the excruciating pain of child-birth but no baby to bring home. I was also looked after by the same nurses who unfortunately remembered me from the year before. To say I was heartbroken was an understatement.

2017 and 2018 will always be difficult years for me as I battled depression, suicidal thoughts, loneliness, and anger as to why my babies kept dying, and yet everyone around me seemed to get pregnant and have their healthy babies. Shame, what was wrong with me?

The thought of getting pregnant again filled me with so much fear as I could not bear to lose another baby. So I did contemplate going for adoption, but then something within me said no, one day you will carry your babies to full term and bring a baby home alive.

And so my husband and I tried again and we found out we were expecting in August 2018.

I was happy but terrified.

This time I was advised to have a cervical stitch in order to hopefully keep my baby inside and prevent preterm labour. I had weekly scans all throughout my pregnancy. I had to be put on bed rest for the last five months of my pregnancy.

Every day was a struggle, but I had to stay positive and have faith that this time things would be different.

And on 13th April 2019 my beautiful baby boy was born, my rainbow after the storm.

Losing a child is not easy; in fact, it's the opposite, it's the most painful thing I have ever experienced, a part of me will always be missing. And yet the babies that I lost have helped to give me a newfound perspective on life, life is to be lived and life truly is a gift. I will always be grateful for my boys, my two precious babies in heaven and the one in my arms here on earth.

There is so much stigma in the Black community surrounding baby loss.

It's often seen as something that you have done; some see it as a spiritual curse or even as some sin that you must have done.

It's something that you are not really allowed to speak on. So often grief is carried out in silence.

You are then expected to move on quickly, as if nothing happened, as if it was not a baby that you had just lost.

It is so important that we continue to have these difficult conversations, in order to properly support those who need it the most.

– Katie Bonful

Throughout this book, I'll be sharing expressions, poems, thoughts, and experiences of other Black pregnant women and mothers whom I have met in person and engaged with through the events, workshops and peer support groups that I have facilitated through The Motherhood Group. I also include words from the mothers who shared with us through our Inquiry into Racial Injustice in Maternity Care led by the Birthrights Charity, of which I am both a Trustee and Co-chair. And I can't forget the wonderful mothers whom I have met virtually, using the powerful tool of the internet and social media.

I want this book to achieve what it's set out to do: not just to amplify my story – I'm merely one Black mother, with one catalogue of a story, one perspective – but to amplify the voices of many other women just like me. Black women are not a monolith: we are multidimensional, multifaceted and multi-layered.

Let's lift the silence. Our voices will collectively echo.

When I got pregnant, I was unprepared for the tsunami of emotions that hit me. On the one hand, I actually was genuinely happy and excited to be having a baby with a man I loved, and I knew that I was going to love my child so much. On the other hand, I was very fearful. I was used to not being a mother, not having a child to look after, not having to alter my routine to accommodate a little one, and certainly not used to anyone relying on me for their very survival. I realized that having a baby was going to throw a grenade into the life I knew; my whole life would change, and nothing would ever be the same again. I realized that far from feeling euphoric and totally unconcerned about any changes that becoming a mother would bring, I did have a lot of thoughts that at the time I felt quite guilty about.

As my pregnancy progressed, there was the strange experience of people giving up their seats for me and smiling at me in the way that people do when they see a pregnant woman, with a mixture of approval and care. So why did I still have this nagging fear? So what, my entire world was going to change – let me just throw myself into motherhood without a backward glance at how my life had been before that. I had no answers to those questions, but I did have a nagging voice in the back of my head that kept on saying things like, 'Your previous life? Oh no, forget about that. Who do you think you are? You are going to be a mother, and that is all that is important now; just dedicate yourself to that like every other good mother does.'

I can remember the day that my contractions started with my first daughter. I was in terrible pain. I rushed to the hospital, but was sent home no fewer than five times, pleading for help only to be turned away. Far from the empathy and compassion that I expected, instead I felt rejected, ignored – as though I was being a nuisance. I honestly tried to rationalize that this was their everyday work; I got that they saw people like me every single day of their working lives in that maternity unit, but as far as I was concerned, I had never been here before. I wanted to be treated with care or, at the very least, respect.

I was dismissed. Eventually, I put my foot down, asserted myself and refused to leave. I tried gas and air, then tried getting into a birthing pool. Time was ticking on, and although I had never expected giving birth to be a walk in the park, it was turning into a nightmare as the hours went by. Eventually, after very many hours of begging for pain relief, I was finally given an epidural. With my second daughter, I was refused painkillers. I cried for an epidural and was told I could handle the pain. Even when her heart rate started to drop. It was only when I felt her head crowning with my own hand that the midwives sprang into action. Chloe was under such a lot of stress that she passed a meconium stool on the way out. I was terrified, traumatized and felt my life was threatened.

When expectations do not match reality

My daughters were born less than two years apart, in the same hospital; there were different staff, but I had the exact same inkling that I was not being listened to on both occasions, that my words were not taken seriously, that I had very little choice. Above all, I was missing the dignity, kindness and respect I had thought would accompany the life-changing experience of bringing a baby into the world. I felt robbed of the 'joyous' experience of giving birth. Ignored. Pain dismissed. Silenced.

Our girls, Zoe and Chloe, were perfect in every way. But my birthing experiences left a very bitter taste in my mouth. What a harsh transition into motherhood.

In the hospital, just after Zoe was born, my husband was told that he had to go. My terror was ramped up tenfold. The only person I trusted in that space wasn't allowed to stay with me. Here I was, after a nightmare labour, feeling even more alone. But to make matters worse, once he left, I was asked to go to the ward clerk's desk. I could barely walk after my epidural, but the staff seemed to think I was strong enough. After all, Black women are strong, right? I had only given birth a few hours earlier, but I managed to hobble to the desk.

At the desk the clerk handed me an envelope. I opened it. It was a letter that was referring me to social services.

I was dumbstruck! Surely, there was some mistake? I had never come in contact with social services or even spoken to a social worker in my entire life. Now, with my daughter just three hours old, I apparently needed to be referred!

'What is this all about?' I asked, trembling.

'I really don't know. I only know that this letter has been attached to your notes.' I was dismissed and sent back to my bed.

Terror almost paralysed me. Were social services coming to take my baby? How could I have done anything wrong? I had literally just given birth.

Once I got home, the social worker duly arrived, and I found out how the referral had come about. As I write this, I'm still shaking my head in disbelief. Years later, I'm still aggrieved, hurt and appalled. It seemed that I had been referred by the community midwife whom I had seen throughout my pregnancy. Retrospectively, I recognized that the midwife had been cold, dismissive and quite rude to me during my appointments. I would try to make a joke to lighten the atmosphere and she would more or less ignore me. *Call the Midwife* it was not! I remember constantly complaining about her to my husband, but I would always be reminded that 'they' just didn't get us – meaning Black people.

The social worker, who was a Black woman, told me that the midwife had said that she suspected my husband was abusing me! That was just so ridiculous it would have been laughable if it had not been so serious. My husband is the kindest and sweetest-natured man you could ever meet.

The social worker apologized several times; she told me what the midwife did was dishonest and wrong. If she had had any suspicion, she was supposed to ask me if I was OK when we were alone, and she could have done that easily because my husband attended only two of my appointments. That's beside the point: nothing remotely like that happened. She judged me and my husband purely on the basis that we were Black.

When the social worker visited, she could see that I was in a loving relationship, that my house was clean, and my daughter very well cared for. Even typing this is making the rage and hurt flood me all over again – why do I have to even justify this entire ordeal? That occasion still haunts me till this very day. Her face expressed everything I felt, and she said verbatim: 'Listen, Sandra, I know exactly what's going on here and I'm sorry that this happened to you.' We both knew what had happened. We both knew that race had everything to do with it.

It was the first time I had been shown any compassion; I felt as if I had been heard, seen and understood. I started crying because we both knew that being a dark-skinned Black woman had everything to do with how I had been treated. The Black social worker advised me to write a letter of complaint, which I did, and as a result the NHS Trust put the midwife who had dealt with me on a training course. They also wrote me a letter of apology.

That was my first step into motherhood, with my first daughter. To make matters worse, with my second birth, this same community midwife came to visit me for my daughter's check-up. I immediately asked for her to be replaced. With not a care in the world, after all of the trauma she had put me through, she had been allowed to come into my space.

It's taken me years to openly speak about this – not even family members know it happened. I still get triggered every time I think about it. But the reason that I am sharing this now is that what happened to me is one of the reasons why many Black women don't ask for help, have a lack of trust in healthcare services and are reluctant to access services for support. For those of us who do ask for help, we will be ignored and dismissed, and for those who are happy minding our own business, we are then judged and never given the benefit of the doubt.

Black women are the group least likely to initiate treatment for postnatal mental illness.[2] Their lack of trust is not groundless. As well as the individual negative experiences, studies have found, again and again, that Black women in the UK are much more likely to die from complications surrounding pregnancy and childbirth than white women; recent studies by MBRRACE-UK, for example, found that Black women in the UK are four times more likely to die than white women when they are having a baby.[3] And when another report on Black maternal deaths appears in the press, it only confirms what we already know: you can literally die by being a Black mother. With that thought alone, how can we not be filled with anxiety and fear throughout our pregnancy and even beyond?

The statistics surrounding Black mothers not accessing perinatal care cannot be adequately addressed without first understanding, then dismantling, racism and bias in the healthcare system.

Structural racism and issues surrounding Black women accessing care had a massive impact on my journey. The UK system is structured such that public policies, institutional practices and cultural representations work to reinforce and perpetuate racial inequity.

Like many other Black women, I chose to struggle on my own and in silence, rather than seek care just for my words to be carelessly taken out of context, to be judged, shown no empathy and then risk having my family torn apart by social services. My concerns have been echoed by several Black women who have shared similar experiences through The Motherhood Group.

We've all been told that it's extremely rare for anyone to die as a result of pregnancy or in childbirth. But after hearing about the figures, I mean it's all out there now, there's no hiding from these frightening stats. I am Black so it is more likely to happen to me. I'll be honest, I didn't really know all of this before I got pregnant and blithely thought that everything would be fine. When I struggled with my mental health after giving birth, I kept it to myself. I was embarrassed and also felt like I could manage on my own.

– Sarah Lawe

There are so many reasons why Black mothers are likely not to seek support and do not receive support, which includes the culture and myth of the 'Strong Black Woman' narrative. This stops so many Black women speaking up more about the issues they face during pregnancy and when they give birth.

Generation after generation, we've been taught to keep quiet about trauma and pain. The belief that a Black woman will not and cannot feel pain as much as white women is ridiculous – and is killing us, literally.

By the year 2024, 75% of Black women will have continuity of care from their midwife throughout their pregnancy, during labour and in the postnatal period.[4] My question is: what *level* of care should be continued throughout? If I was promised the same midwife who was cold and treated me differently because of my race, throughout my pregnancy, labour and postnatal period, that would have been a nightmare come true.

My own experience was a huge wake-up call. My midwife had shown me no warmth as a new mother-to-be, or even as another empathetic woman; instead, she had judged me from the colour of my skin and extended the judgement to my husband. She had arrived at the conclusion that I was not a fit mother – based on what, exactly?

Very early on in my motherhood journey, I felt that I could never ever trust healthcare professionals.

I was not in a position to be strong. I had no time for myself, caring for this beautiful little baby 24/7, cooking and cleaning as if my life depended on it, determined to be absolutely perfect and get everything absolutely right. And not only did I have to prove it to the Nigerian aunties and other members of the family, but I was determined to show that midwife that she had made the biggest mistake of her life. I was so focused on 'proving' to myself that I was a 'Nneoma', the good mother, that I ignored the signs and my needs.

It was a lot of pressure and hardly the blissful transition to motherhood that I had hoped for. I was drowning in it all and I suffered in silence.

My initial interactions with maternity services reeked of un-conscious biases and, at the time, I didn't have the voice to speak up and to speak my truth – the unwritten rule of not being able to share my pain and how I was feeling. I was scared to say that I no longer felt like Sandra Igwe, that confident girl, exuberating boldness, basking in self-assurance. She was gone.

Dare I say to my family or my friends that I was struggling and that I needed support? My husband was super supportive but he just could never understand the shift that I was going through emotionally and physically; my body had changed as well.

Now I was refusing to answer my phone to people, just letting it ring out. How could I let people know I didn't sound like my normal self? Instagram, Twitter, Snapchat – I switched off. Why would I want to watch people 'living their best life', as we like to put it, when I was going through depression? Blinds closed, TV off, room dark at 2pm in the afternoon. Just me and my precious baby, sadness, joy, isolation, unconditional love...it was all so confusing for me. Motherhood – an oxymoron for many of us: the sadness and joy, feeling isolated yet having unconditional love; losing yourself slowly, while finding your new self daily.

I took small walks, which did help, but for the most part, I hid. When anyone asked if I was okay, my instant response was, 'Oh yeah, sure, I'm fine!' My go-to answer for everyone and anyone. Even when the midwife would come around, she'd ask me her standard tick-box questions and I would force a smile and respond, 'Oh yes, I'm fine, everything is fine, fine, fine!' It's not as if she genuinely cared about how I was actually feeling anyway, I thought. As she read the questions from her paper, in her fast robotic monotone, which were mainly about my daughter anyway, I just knew she wouldn't care. Secretly, in hindsight, I wish she would have looked me deep in my eyes, filled with sadness, and asked if I was genuinely coping, asked if I was happy, asked if I felt alone. Typing this now, my eyes are filled with tears, because that's all I really wanted. Someone to pick up that I was desperately but silently screaming for help. Why was it so hard for them to see through my mask?

It was an ongoing theme, with me telling everybody what they ultimately wanted to hear, that I was 'fine'. But once the door was shut, and it was just us, though I still felt alone, I would cry, for hours.

That's when I started Googling my symptoms: 'mum, crying,

sad, new mum, depressed'. The more I read, the more I understood; the more I understood, the more in denial I was. Could it be 'baby blues', 'postnatal depression', 'postnatal anxiety'? But it couldn't be.

I didn't see myself as a depressed person. I was bubbly, the life and soul of the party, and as well as that, I'm a Nigerian woman. Nigerians, Africans, Black people – we're strong! I broke down. The more I tried to cloak myself in denial, the more I knew I was lying to myself.

As ignorant and simple-minded as this sounds, I grew up believing 'Mental Health' was a 'white person's issue', and unfortunately many Black people had this mindset for a very long time – some still do. In many parts of Africa, people still believe that the idea of depression is an excuse, that the 'white man' made it up. And if the only scale for mental health applied to the crazy person running around, butt naked, then it's clear they have lost their mind.

Surely, though, perinatal health challenges couldn't apply to someone like me, someone who was able to keep the house spotlessly clean, cook, dress up, smile, iron and look after the baby so well – in fact, do everything that was required of me. But it *was* me, and that was the start of my undiagnosed postnatal depression journey.

Gone with the milk

Crying in the shower
Watching the glass steam up
And the world disappear
At least I can't see my reflection in the mirror
Small victories!
Large stretch marks
Thighs as big as my misery
A healing scar hidden by pubic hair
As wild as the hair on my head

And just as matted!

This is the only place that I can be alone
I fall apart
Watch my life circle at my feet
Before being sucked down the drain
Where is the joy I was promised?

Feeling sorry for myself
Feeling guilty because I can't even seem to muster a smile
All the while I'm being mummy

So I am in the shower
Spending ten minutes by myself
The water hot enough to scour and scold the skin
But what soap washes away depression?
Thumbs up anyway, at least I've washed today.
Small victories!
It's been a year and it's only getting worse
Back to work
Trapped by my responsibilities
No fun, no laughter, just emotional mental rants
Sweets, chocolate digestive, fried chicken and stretchy pants
BBQ ribs by the rack
Trying to find comfort in food but the food don't hug back

Doing all I have to do, being who I have to be
A professional, a wife, and still someone's mummy
Whilst mourning for the loss of the woman I used to be
Having arguments with my dad because he's not sure that
    breast is best
And I'm crying because I just want to get some rest
So I use formula because I believe that could be the solution

But I start falling out of love with her and me
Hence the confusion
She's lying here with her head on my chest
We are no longer connected by the breast
I stroke the hair on her head, it's like silk
I realize the last ounce of joy I had just dried up with my milk.

– *Lucy Zion*

Dear Dark Days

Dear Dark Days, stark days, empty and vast, cry the whole day away, days.

I just thought you should know what I'm doing now.

I am a woman who is no longer ashamed to admit that I didn't at first fit seamlessly into motherhood and that sleepless nights made me feel deprived of my own life. I am a mother who spends a lot of time reassuring myself that we all make mistakes, and that good days can outweigh the bad. I ask for help when I need it and I am not afraid to say I need a little time for myself when I feel it is all getting a little too much.

I just thought you should know how I'm feeling.

I am impressed by how depressed you had me being, how isolated you had me from those who gave my life meaning. How scared I was to confess that I wasn't the best I had ever been.

Because before you, I was constantly achieving all that I was dreaming for. And yet somehow you had me believing that I was unworthy of receiving the blessings I had been praying for.

I just thought you should know what I have been through.

Since the last time I saw you, I found my way through the night, without a single star in the sky to guide me. You haunted my every step and I heard your laughter on the wind as you patronized my efforts to find me. You hid my joy from me. You hid my own voice from me.

That time I trusted in myself enough to know I wasn't well and that I needed help with my mental health was especially important to me.

I just thought you should know what I wish for the future.

I hope that the mountains you made me climb to get my mind right, have prepared me for battles that I will stand victoriously in and slay the darkness that comes from within. I have walked through the valley of the shadow of depression, so why would I fear death or dying?

I just thought you should know what I don't miss about you.

I am glad I don't have to worry about if today will be the day I end my life, if today I will stop being a mother and a wife, if I will submit to depression and give in to the strife, I don't worry about that anymore.

I just thought you should know what I miss a lot.

I miss the way you used to cuddle me in bed, hold me there, screening the anxieties in my head, I was comforted by your numbness and rejected people for loneliness instead. I miss this like I'd miss a hole in my head.

I just thought you should know that.

Peace out! No longer yours.

– Lucy Zion

Black women are meant to have it all figured out

The journey of being a Black mother in the UK has been an ever-moving scale of extremes for me. From feeling as though I have it all figured out and have a nice pace and balance in place, to feeling as though I have absolutely no clue what to do, say or feel and at times even helpless. Considering that before this time, I had only experienced being a daughter, sister, aunty, cousin, friend, girlfriend and colleague, the expectation to have this side of me (a brand-new Black mother raised in the UK by a single mother who was born and raised in a country with ways that at times conflict with those where we currently lay our head) all figured out laid heavy on my shoulders. Why? Because for whatever reason, Black women are meant to have it all figured out in any area of their life, right?!

From the moment I found out I was pregnant, my mind was flooded with questions, thoughts and feelings that I never even knew existed but have now become a part of my reality. Such as:

'What school will fully accept my daughter's heritage and also help to nurture this element of her?'

'Will the doctor take my cry for help as seriously as I know they need to regarding my child's health and wellbeing?'

'Is this the right age for my daughter to have extensions in her hair or will I be seen as a lazy mother who does not want to bother doing her daughter's hair (because as much as I love doing her hair and as beautiful as her hair may be, the struggle is real in trying to fit in hair maintenance for a child with thick curly and easily knotty hair as a full-time working single parent)?'

'How and when do I explain racism to her (as unfortunately this is something that she is more than likely going to experience from being in the UK as a Black girl)? And what do I teach her in regard to how to deal with it (especially as there are many layers to racism)?'

'Should we travel to [insert country here] or will the trip be more consumed with defending our existence as human beings who were born with heavily melanated skin?'

'Am I spoiling her too much because I'm trying to give her everything I never had, as well as trying to make up for what I cannot give her?'

'Am I teaching her all she needs in order to manoeuvre in this colourful world safely (as I know her journey will be different from those who do not look like her)?'

'How can I help her to not be so heavily affected by the fact that she is now being raised in a single-parent household?'

All these questions, which really and truly do not necessarily have a concrete and complete definitive answer, suddenly became the dialogue my mind would have with my morals, culture, societal pressures and more.

Motherhood for me started from the moment I saw the blue lines on the pregnancy test. Since then, every decision I have had to make has been filtered through the lens of being someone's mum. But not only someone's mum, someone's young Black mum in a country that at times can feel as though you do not belong. This means that my experience of motherhood, as a Black woman, can only conjure up sympathy from mothers who do not come from the same background as myself. Sympathy in the sense of understanding what it is like to have to do night feeds, deal with the terrible twos (which no one tells you starts from before they are two by the way), teething, getting used to your new mum body and more.

– *Yvonne Ihegborow*

I believed that until I became a wife, my life was under-achieved

When I became a solo parent, I had to deal with a lot of noise from other people that didn't always reflect how I felt about myself. Comments such as 'Oh no, you're a single mum, I can't believe you're doing it alone.' Or 'I can't imagine how it feels that you're a single parent, how will you cope?' I found these comments to be patronizing and didn't want people to treat me like an alien or like I had an illness. 'Being a single mum is not an illness.' Because I felt alone in my situation and confused about my future, I had overwhelming feelings of guilt about the situation I had put my children in. I felt fear and worry and, at times, definitely felt that I was the living embodiment of people's negative perceptions and the stereotype society sees as a Black single mum.

I eventually realized that these negative labels and associations from our communities were not how I wanted to see myself. Changing my narrative around this involved letting go of the constant mum guilt about my situation and refusing to be shamed by it.

Mum guilt mainly stems from outside influences and expectations we put on ourselves.

Single mums feel shame and are often judged, but interestingly dads are not criticized in the same way. When my relationship broke down, I remember that it took me time to let people know about it because I felt embarrassed that we were no longer together, especially being a mother of two and already having experienced being on my own with my first child. Once I realized that the relationship would inevitably come to an end, how I acted from this point equipped me with the tools needed, and I began to let go of the guilt I felt. I was determined not to be another stereotype and would prove it to people by my actions and the type of parent I would be to my children. As mums, we will always feel guilty about something, whether it's forgetting our children's 'own clothes day' at school so our son or daughter is the only one in their class in school uniform. Or any of the other dozens of things that we have to remember daily. What we are doing constantly and consistently is making decisions that are child-centred and we shouldn't feel guilty if we are doing our best. I used to believe that until I became a wife and got married that my life was under-achieved, especially because the magazines and social media all show you what motherhood goals should look like. There was a time when I would attend parents' evening and look around and see everywhere two parents sitting together waiting to talk to their child's teacher and there was me sitting on my lonesome thinking and feeling so ashamed and guilty. The reality is I don't know what goes on behind closed doors and acceptance was what I had to do to enable me to just settle my mind and stop thinking about what was out of my control.

As a mother who is raising my son and daughter on my own, my mission to establish healthy co-parenting effectively with the focus on the child's needs is a real challenge, especially when communication between the father of my son and me is not in a good place. I have found the absence and periodic contact of my son's father to be extremely disruptive to establishing a routine. I now have had to explore other ways to ensure that my children are receiving positive adult influences in their lives and having their needs met. For example, in the past, I have looked to other adults in my extended family or community to help me manage my son's considerable energy levels. I realized that he needs a male influence to help me understand more about his needs, and as a solo parent, I need a break from them both at times to give me some headspace. One bit of advice I would give to single mums is: Do not be afraid to pick up the phone and ask for help; respite from your children when you need to recharge your batteries is vital for your mental wellbeing.

I am managing my son's expectations around the contact with his father in age-appropriate conversations and have been accessing support from CAMHS (Child and Adolescent Mental Health Services) plus receiving support from his school to help me and him during this difficult period. The school and other professionals have been very non-judgemental and I have been very transparent in explaining our current situation.

Being honest with your child and his school allows them to have an insight into what he is facing emotionally and provide him with interventions that will help him to regulate his feelings and emotions.

I am doing the best I can to facilitate relationships with a child-centred approach to parenting, to provide a balanced effort on both sides. In addition to the conversations I have had with my son, I have also been keeping a diary via email by writing emails addressed to my son. These are factual and non-judgemental, for my son to read when he is older.

– Fiona Small

CHAPTER 2

When Lack of Trust Stops You Asking for Help

The doorbell rang and I tried to push down tears. I was so angry and hurt. I'd just gone through a difficult birth, and now...? This is it, I thought. *Social services can take my daughter from me for absolutely no reason.*

I'd never come up against any institutional trouble before, but now, because my midwife decided that my husband was dangerous, because he was a big Black man, I had to let a social worker into our untroubled home to judge my parental fitness. *How is this possibly allowed?* I thought. It all seemed beyond crazy and bizarre. We were two well-educated, honest adults who wanted to start our family in peace.

Why do we have to prove ourselves just because of our melanated skin?

When I opened the door, I let out a long sigh. The social worker was a Black woman. *Thank you, God*, I prayed. I smiled. 'Please, come in.'

We sat down, I offered her tea, we had a conversation, and we tried in earnest to understand why this interaction was even happening in the first place. 'I have no idea where she got the idea that my husband is abusive. He is the complete opposite!' I shook my head in disbelief that I was even having this conversation. 'The midwife seemed really cold. I don't think she liked us at all. And she definitely didn't seem as if she was concerned or cared for my wellbeing...' I was genuinely confused. As someone who thought I was being harmed, shouldn't she have at least cracked a smile at me, spoken to me with warmth and asked me how my day was? I wasn't buying this abuse baloney – she was racist and was moved to act in a discriminatory way because we were Black. End of.

The social worker smiled, then looked up at me with understanding eyes. 'I know what's going on here,' she said. 'Your midwife should have spoken to you directly if she genuinely feared for your safety. That's part of our general procedure.'

We looked at each other, two Black women on either side of the system, both trying to do right by my child. We knew what racism looked like. We had navigated white women and their feelings our whole lives. We understood that the midwife had made an assumption about Black men and Black mothers. She held my hand and apologized while saying that she was closing the case immediately.

After the social worker left, I sat on the sofa for a few minutes, in silence.

In my silence, I was grateful, but numb. What would have happened if someone else had come to the door? Would Zoe have been whisked away to social care? Would this have been escalated? Would the person not have believed my words – me as a mother? Zoe, possibly taken from me, a mother who loved her and could care for her? How many other Black women experience this same type of unnecessary and undue trauma?

Have you ever heard the saying by R.M. Williams, 'Trust is the easiest thing in the world to lose, and the hardest thing in the world to get back'? Well, how do I put this? Many of us Black women have trust issues. With healthcare professionals, maternity and mental health services – heck, the entire 'system'! I know I certainly did, and if I'm being honest, I still do. And rightly so.

In the UK, postnatal depression affects more than one in every ten women within a year of giving birth,[5] added to which Black women have a higher burden of mental health disorders when compared with white women.[6] And if that isn't bad enough, we're less likely to have these disorders treated or even detected for that matter...

I only found out these statistics well after the birth of both my daughters, Zoe and Chloe. And if someone asked me how I felt initially hearing this, what would I have said? Horrified? Yes. Melancholy? Absolutely, but shocked? Of course not – let's be real. I'll share more about why we're less likely to have our symptoms treated in the next chapter, but let us address why many of us don't actually *want* to be identified as depressed and why we were not necessarily perceived as depressed in our pregnancy or postpartum period. I want to make this clear: the blame and onus should not – I repeat, should not – be placed on a Black mother as to why these horrifying statistics mainly affect us, but it's crucial to acknowledge and recognize other factors that impact why many Black women like me just cannot bring ourselves forward to ask for support.

As I know all too well, untreated postpartum depression can and does have a severe impact on the health and wellbeing of any woman, and it will always remain a dark period of my life. So why on earth would I *not* want to reach out, ask for support and let healthcare professionals – those who were in the *best* position to potentially do so – help me?

One thing that is typically suggested in any mental illness, from depression to the severe postnatal depression that I suffered, is that speaking to someone you can trust can be the first step to getting the help you need. But what happens when you don't or can't trust?

In my case, once I realized that there was something wrong, I was too afraid to share how I was feeling. Given the fact that I had a brush with social services early on, entirely unwarranted though it had proven to be, I still feared that if I said anything at all, the next step would be for social services to get involved and swoop down to take my precious daughter away from me. What I felt was about as far from 'trust' as you could get. In my case, and for many other Black women, it felt like 'us' versus 'them'. As if we were not on the same team, not fighting for the same cause. Almost as if we were in a secret battle where Black women have been losing for years. On what grounds could we possibly be persuaded to trust?

Even if a Black person does get a mental health diagnosis, we are much more likely to end up with poor treatment outcomes, and the result of that is often disengagement from mainstream mental health services. Trust issues naturally lead to disengagement. And it doesn't take a professor to know this.

All of this begins to build a picture of the difficulties in engaging with mental health services if you are a Black woman, or Black full stop. Listening to and reading hundreds of Black mothers' experiences, as outrageous as they were, I wasn't surprised at all, but the more I researched, listened, heard and saw through my advocacy work, the more I became aware of that sinking feeling in the pit of my stomach.

Can you imagine having the same ailments as a white person but experiencing a significantly different mental healthcare pathway? This is exactly what has happened in the UK. What this means is that some Black people are less likely even to get a referral to mental health services through their GP. But it also – chillingly – means that we're more likely to be arrested by the police following a crisis, even if it was triggered by a mental health issue; we're more likely to be seen as antisocial, or even criminal, than our white counterparts. Essentially, therefore, it is not *that* bizarre for me to say that as a Black mother, with perinatal mental health issues, the fear of feeling on the brink of being criminalized for merely struggling as a new mother is justifiable.

It goes without saying that this will inevitably result in poorer health outcomes and often coercive forms of care in locked wards. So, knowing all this, and being aware of these disparities, I realized that there was something about the whole system that was deeply inequitable. My own experience, although very distressing, I very soon realized, was not unusual. We as Black people often don't trust healthcare services – and by that I mean not just maternity services but *all* the services, across the board – and the reason for this becomes very clear. It is as simple as Black people knowing through their own experience, or that of others, that the services offer a long history of not putting Black people's best interests at the forefront.

Speaking on trust, in today's world, it's complex. Everyone and everything is fast and constantly changing. Slightly off topic, but still appropriate, you only have to read the sad statistics about old people being scammed by conniving criminals on the phone, women being cheated out of money by men they've met on online dating sites, businesses that take your money then fail to come up with the goods...you name it – the term *caveat emptor* (buyer beware) has never been more relevant. The old moral codes that once kept most of us in check seem, for the most part, to have been blown away.

Trust is earned.

Funnily enough, a Mori poll[7] stated that the 'public' trusts doctors more than any other professional group. You might be wondering why I chose to write 'public' in inverted commas – well, I'm not convinced that this public represents Black women fairly. However, according to this poll, more than nine in ten members of the public (92%) have faith in doctors. To tell the truth, right now as I type this, I'm side-eyeing frantically.

From my personal experience, there have been many

contributing factors that have accelerated my lack of trust not just in medics but in the entire healthcare system, especially during my pregnancy and postpartum period.

The questions below have raced uncontrollably through my mind not just as a Black pregnant woman but a Black woman in general:

Do they understand, recognize or even acknowledge racism?

How can I trust them when they don't even seem like they actually care?

If they don't see me as a multifaceted Black woman, with valid feelings, can I open up to them?

Their actions and unresponsiveness to my concerns suggest that they lack empathy and accountability. Do they have my best interest at heart?

They haven't asked about my faith. Are they bothered about me?

They keep referring to me as aggressive and angry. Can I share my truth with them?

If I tell them I'm concerned or in pain, will they even believe me?

I feel invisible, stereotyped and a non-priority. What's the point?

When I went into labour the first time, I desperately wanted to be naked. I was in so much pain that I just couldn't bear the feeling of fabric on my skin. Wasn't that how women had given birth for thousands of years? Why wear clothes?

I pulled my gown off to focus on breathing through the pain. 'Sandra,' scolded a nurse, 'put that back on. You can't just be topless. What if we have to wheel you into another room?'

I'm giving birth! I wanted to shout. *Who cares if someone sees my naked breasts?*

As the hours dragged on, I tried again. *I don't give a heck*, I thought. *This is too much fabric.*

Again, the nurses pulled my gown back on. 'Can't have that, Sandra.'

I realized the nurses viewed me as a challenging Black woman, someone to be controlled rather than cared for. Even during birth, I was expected to maintain poise and decorum to keep others at ease. *Don't be too much. Don't be too loud. Too upset.* Why didn't they realize that I was in too much pain to care about decorum?

It's almost as if a request coming from a Black woman is automatically seen as 'challenging', or perhaps they aren't used to respecting and listening to our desires – like 'How dare you ask for what you want!'

Ultimately, although no one held a gun to my head, I was forced to be uncomfortable, to wear my garment unwillingly. Many of you might think, 'So what?' But for me, as a Black mother, it only reinforced what I already felt. That I didn't matter. My choices didn't matter. I had no autonomy over my own body.

Ignoring Black mothers has an adverse effect not only on *our* wellbeing but also on the health of our children. When my second daughter Chloe was six months old, she stopped growing. 'She looks small,' I told my health visitor. 'Could she be sick?'

'Don't be so dramatic,' said the woman, rolling her eyes. 'She's perfectly normal.'

I looked at my beautiful daughter. She seemed weak, not just delicate. *I don't think this is normal*, I thought.

'I didn't see the health visitor write Chloe's weight down in the red book,' I told my husband later that evening.

'Isn't that part of their job?' he asked.

Chloe got weaker and weaker. My precious baby didn't seem like the same baby I had held a few weeks back. I was breast-feeding day and night, hoping that she would get bigger. What was happening? Why wouldn't anybody help me? My concerns were dismissed, ignored; I was told that I was just an 'over-worried mum'.

When doctors finally diagnosed Chloe with rickets, I was furious. The doctor who initially saw Chloe was shocked as he read her vitamin D count aloud, in disbelief; he also said, 'I didn't think children *got* rickets any more.' He shook his head. 'There's just not enough sunlight in England for someone with your daughter's complexion. She doesn't absorb vitamin D as easily. You need to give her supplements.'

When I told the ladies at my church about Chloe's situation for moral support, rather than shocked indignation, many of them responded with similar stories. 'That happened to my sister-in-law's son,' one aunty said. 'We started keeping my granddaughter out in the sun as much as possible,' said another.

It seemed as if every woman I spoke to had another sad tale about someone she knew whose baby had suffered from this supposedly old-world condition. Why was this not being shouted from the rooftops? Why didn't nurses take every single Black mother in the UK aside to relay this crucial information?

How am I supposed to ever trust healthcare providers after this? I wondered.

After almost a year of perplexity, I found the courage to seek justice for Chloe. On 4 November 2019, I wrote a letter of complaint to the NHS Trusts Locality Manager: 'Dear XXXX, I wish to pursue a claim in relation to the lack of treatment carried out and negligent care provided by the designated health visitor...' For legal reasons, I cannot disclose more details as my daughter's case is still ongoing; however, I can share that the Trust has so far admitted to a breach of duty of care.

Do you see how difficult it is to trust a system that seems like it was designed to mishandle Black women?

Trust has to be earned.

The journey to services earning the trust of Black women starts off with first having the desire to actually want to be trusted. That's a given, but ultimately, some of us even wonder, do they even care if we ever get the support in maternal mental health services or not? Once there is a hunger to see change, and a desire to close the gaps in understanding, you have to understand that culture plays a part in our experiences – don't tell me you 'do not see colour'. First, know that I am Black; see me, see me as I am. Know that stigma plays a part, as well as language, my faith, family structure and dynamic. For example, in many African and Caribbean households, the role of a mother, even a woman, plays a vital position in providing care and security while nurturing the entire family. Very often, Black women's options for self-reflection and comfort may be limited due to the expectations placed upon them. And so, for many of us, it's customary to prioritize the wellbeing and interests of our families over our own. Understanding this is an important step to show that you have a genuine interest in us.

Black women would trust more if we saw better representation in healthcare governance structures, senior leadership positions – heck, even if we saw more of ourselves reflected in marketing materials, or if our language was in literature. When was the last time you saw Igbo, Yoruba, Twi or Lingala as a translation option? Never. Why aren't healthcare services connecting with real, local and diverse organizations and community groups that are already interacting with us?

Trust has to be earned, not freely given.

How can a mother freely give up her trust, truly be herself, when she's not even asked about her cultural and faith needs – a core element that affects virtually every aspect of my life, but which isn't even taken into consideration, let alone acknowledged? Why would I trust when I believe race influenced my treatment while giving birth and afterwards? If I felt extremely unsafe during my maternity care – was ignored, disbelieved, disrespected, coerced into interventions and a recipient of microaggressions – why would I then go on to speak about my mental health after? Begging for hours for pain relief, and not being given any because I 'looked like I could handle it', pleading and hoping that my cries would stir up some sort of hidden sympathy, exhausted, I lost the one crumb of trust I had for maternity services.

Trust can be given.

Being a British-born Nigerian means I'm layered with heaps of rich culture, traditions and practices that often guide the way I want to receive care and, many times, understand care. But if healthcare services sincerely want change, the full onus should not be on me, the mum, in a vulnerable position of new motherhood to bend, conform and submit to the white man's rules and regulations, figuratively and literally. Let's at least meet halfway. Healthcare professionals should try to understand at the very least that a Black mother's engagement in accessing services significantly reflects the level of understanding shown towards her culture – which makes up who she is. Don't reject or make me believe that my culture is less significant. Prior to the pandemic, why was the practice of African women coming collectively to visit a new mother frowned upon? Why should we have to explain the significance of this cultural practice?

If you observe my cultural norms, social expectations, traditions – even something as simple as getting my name right – I'm more likely to open up and feel relaxed, which ultimately leads to better trust. And where this is ignored, I would not have the boldness and self-assurance to interact effectively with services.

Get my name right

It's subtle,
It's covert, it's not really in your face –
It's hard to describe
You can't really explain it

Nor can you really describe it, but you can feel it.
And you know it when it's done to you, and once you've
    experienced it.
Not getting my name right,
I know my name may seem hard to somebody who doesn't
    speak the Igbo language.
Learning is a sign of care.
But learning how to get someone's name right is the first step to:
Showing that you want to respect them,
Showing that you actually care about the person you're
    speaking with,
Engaging with,
Dealing with.
Practise how to get my name right.

– Sandra Igwe

Black motherhood and trust in the healthcare system

It is hard to trust a healthcare system where Black women are four times more likely to suffer maternal death than a white woman. Data and stats do not lie. No person should have to think, am I going to die because of the colour of my skin? I feel like my life is not prioritized. I feel like my life is not valued. I feel like my life is not important in the eyes of the healthcare system. I was relieved when I did not have a girl, as I did not want her to have the same fate. To be a potential statistic.

– *Anonymous*

Black motherhood and healthcare. The two terms feel almost paradoxical. Every Black mother I know has a wealth of negative experiences with the 'healthcare system'. 'Wealth' and 'negative' – now that's paradoxical. The feeling of having to defend yourself whenever you are in pain, championing the right to live and being told to stop exaggerating are among some of these experiences.

The very people who are meant to care for us are the very people who perpetuate a system of carelessness when it concerns Black women. The healthcare system is to Black women as the judicial system is to Black men. 'Four times more likely [to die in childbirth].' That's the statistic. Let that sink in. That is not due to the fact that medicines and procedures don't work for Black mothers.

It's because of the simple fact that the healthcare system is actually an institutionalized racist system.

– Trevona

My son was born at 32 weeks.

When my waters broke, I went straight to the hospital. When I arrived, I was seen shortly after. I was told that it was just thrush (I was 26 and knew exactly what thrush was). I was sent home with a pad and told to come back if it filled up.

I came back later that day and was greeted very rudely by a nurse who asked me for the used pads as she needed proof. She then left me in a room for three hours. The doctor who finally came to check me was in shock. 'Oh shit, you were right,' he said. I was then admitted straight away but it was now 10.30pm so there was no one to book me in. After three days I gave birth to my son. I didn't get to hold him as he was rushed off to a team of doctors. The next time I saw him was three hours later. He was in the neonatal intensive unit with tubes in his nose. He stayed for almost four weeks. During this time the nurses were very cold and condescending towards me. After 17 days my son took part in a voluntary MRI scan where we found that he had a stroke. I have gotten different stories about how it happened. He now has mild cerebral palsy.

– Anisha Maragera

It's impossible to place trust in a system that is committed to letting you down. You don't realize how much you need a stable and reliable healthcare system until you're in the very vulnerable state of pregnancy. Until then, you're questioning whether it's the system that killed your babies or your own incompetent body.

When I was pregnant with my son, I found myself having to lean on a system I wasn't sure could support me and my baggage, my fears, my history and my questions.

'Are you sure I'll be OK?'

'Is my baby going to be fine this time around?'

'What will be different this time around?'

It didn't help that we were in the throes of a pandemic and the headline at the time was the mortality rate of Black women giving birth. Thankfully, I crossed the threshold of my house with a live baby in my hands (this time around). Yes, my trust in the healthcare system was shaky but...

– Madeline

Dismissed and ignored

I remember on both occasions, I made requests, pleaded and cried to my midwife for pain relief. Especially with my second daughter, Chloe, I knew exactly what I wanted: epidural. I didn't want to endure the 37 hours of pain I went through with my first daughter. But despite asking and begging for pain relief, I didn't get any. I was dismissed, ignored and told I was in somewhat of a 'queue' for pain relief. Personally, I knew my race had everything to do with why

I was treated in this manner. Before you ask, 'How do you know you weren't given pain relief because you're Black?'– well, studies find that a Black patient with the same level of pain and everything else being accounted for is much less likely to receive pain relief than a white patient with the same characteristics.[8]

Growing up, I was raised to believe that having a submissive approach when engaging with healthcare professionals would make me less intimidating, and therefore I would be more likely to receive better care. But I only now see that this mindset, which many of us may have had, was harmful, resulting in Black women being reluctant to question information and advice, and, of course, igniting uncertainty. Now imagine not being able to speak English as an additional layer and barrier. I can only envisage further disproportionate treatment. Not understanding recommendations, not being able to attend further appointments because of misunderstanding, not feeling comfortable to say what you are really feeling because of the simplest misinterpretation. The list goes on. But yet such mothers don't get additional time and aren't listened to.

I know that if healthcare professionals understood cultural factors and sensitivities that affected Black women and mothers, our care as a whole would be a lot less daunting. Whether you call it conscious or unconscious bias, covert or overt racism – others might call it pure ignorance – addressing this is the first step to better care for Black women.

One of the many reasons, as I mentioned, that many Black women don't want any connection with mental health and the challenges that come with it is the language that's used. It tends to be extremely stigmatizing and taboo, especially for an African or a Caribbean person who may have grown up in a household that believed 'mental health' is a white man's disease.

I know that the maternity services that interacted with me, and with the many, many other women I have spoken to, were not inquisitive. Not in a nosey, interrogative way. But in a caring, curious and thoughtful manner. Thinking inclusively and exploratively about my family dynamic, taking time out to understand my family's culture, structure and thoughts around perinatal mental health disorders and services. No one asked me genuine questions, about my social network, why I had moved out of London to another city, how that impacted me, if I went to church, and overall my involvement with maternity services. Maybe then they would have known that my traumatic birthing experience had almost crippled me, emotionally, that I was struggling with isolation and loneliness, and that one of my main sources of comfort was, in fact, my faith.

Open questions would have paved the way for dialogues, for a conversation that would have led to smiles and tears, and maybe got closer to the truth. But my answers were short and sharp, just like their tick-boxed questions – not even about me, but my baby. If only my health visitor had warmly asked about my husband, she would have learnt that I missed him badly because he worked very long hours, and that at the time it felt like I was basically a single mother. All they knew was that Mrs Sandra Igwe was a married woman, a happily married woman – at least based on the photos they saw in my house. And, sadly, in no way did they involve my partner, as if I had created our child on my own.

They might have found out that Zoe only liked the taste of breastmilk, but hated actually breastfeeding, and so I had to pump every two hours, every single day – even through the night – and this was literally crushing my spirit and sanity, which impacted my relationship with my husband, and I was spiralling further into the depressed ocean that was consuming me. My husband had no clue what perinatal mental health issues looked like, but he was in the best position to support me, and yet no one spoke about him or to him. If he had known about the signs and symptoms, the treatment options available and what they involved, positive outputs and negative effects, what recovery and prevention might look like, he would have definitely been my reassuring saving grace. But he was not even considered a factor.

Why was no one asking me these crucial questions?

The health visitor knew I was new to the area but did not ask if that was difficult because my family and friends could not just randomly drive 200 miles to visit me and my new baby. She knew my house was clean and tidy but didn't know that my anxiety and painful experience with social services drew me onto the horrid path of perfectionism, so every aspect of my home, parenting and life had to be in a strict place. She knew I was Black African, not just by the way I looked and my answers to tick-boxed questions on countless documents, but she didn't know I was a Black British woman, whose parents were Igbo, and my identity was a kaleidoscope of eastern Nigerian culture, originally living in a South London environment and now moved to another city. And that, essentially, I had no one to turn to for authentic, non-judgemental support, or so I felt at one point.

If she had asked me about me, and listened, I would have felt more inclined to ask my own questions, therefore building trust.

Language is such a powerful tool

Through language we can inform, influence, persuade, coerce, deceive, negotiate, manipulate, gossip, hurt, or comfort. Language can also be used to destigmatize, welcome and create a better understanding of mental health in the Black community.

Personally, I prefer the term 'positive wellbeing' over mental health.

When you look at the word 'mental', there's a long history of the slang term being used to describe 'crazy' or 'delirious'. Who wants to be associated with such a negative connotation?

I remember coming to terms with the fact that I probably had postnatal depression and anxiety after giving birth. I mean all the signs and symptoms were there. But just saying the words to my family, 'I think I'm *depressed*; I think I'm going through *mental health* issues', I used to almost whisper the words. As if it was my dirty little secret. Forbidden words. Filled with muck and filth – so I thought at the time. I don't think I ever recall my mother or father speaking about mental health as such. It was a new concept, and, arguably, is still a new concept within certain communities. I felt disconnected from the word itself.

Cultural consideration of language, as a full concept, builds trust.

Out of frustration and a desperate need for my experiences to be validated, heard and understood, I created essentially my own form of support. Now, looking back, it was a radical type of peer support tailored to my specific needs as a new Black mother. I eventually set up a social enterprise, The Motherhood Group, which started off as a WhatsApp group for new mothers and pregnant women who were all Black. We all shared our most honest experiences, thoughts and challenges with each other, and I couldn't believe that my feelings for the first time felt not only normalized but also validated. It was as if I cured myself of the shame, guilt, isolation and stigma that embodied me, simply by speaking to other mothers who 'got it' – not having to explain myself, second-guess my circumstances. Mostly, I laughed again and found comfort in what I now understand was my community.

The mums in The Motherhood Group reassured me that my current situation would pass, and although most of our conversations happened virtually, I felt a warm sense of support. Our first ever meet-up had more than 70 mothers attending – the venue reached capacity. Mums just like me drove miles and miles, just so that we could continue such vital conversations. It was and still is our safe space. For the most part, that was our only sense of a social life at that time.

After so many events, meet-ups and workshops hosted by The Motherhood Group, I got a clearer understanding of the common themes that arose from thousands of Black mothers, which has given me the confidence to write this book.

Although Black women and our experiences are not monolithic, we can't deny that we're often singing our melodic song from the same hymn sheet, especially when it comes to our interactions with maternity and mental health services.

At the back of the queue

You ask any Black person and they will tell you that they have felt the sting of disrespect, sometimes on a daily basis, purely on the basis that they are Black.

Black is glorious.

I often have to remind myself of that because society will make you feel otherwise. Many Black people will tell you that they feel acutely disrespected in their everyday lives, discrimination that they – and yes, I too – have experienced as both subtle and, at other times, quite explicit. A Black woman, like me, or a Black man – in fact, anyone Black – will be able to tell you all you want to know about everyday racism. This mistrust starts from each time you leave the house, get shoved out of the way in the bus queue, or enter a shop where someone else is served before you. Or should I say *someone white* is served before you? I could give you a hundred examples; any Black person could.

I have heard so many Black people talk about discriminatory experiences they have within the mental health system. My own experience makes me unsurprised that many have expressed dissatisfaction with mental health services, given the fact that there is the tendency, with a Black patient, to over-diagnose. The result of this can often be a truly terrifying admission to a medium-security or even a high-security psychiatric ward or clinic, and much less emphasis placed on offering a Black person psychologically based intervention.

So, knowing this, how would I ever think it was a good idea to talk to any of these 'professionals'? If I said anything about feeling low or even mildly depressed, would they class me as an unhinged lunatic, throw me into a mental facility and take my child away from me completely?

The very thought of it made me go cold as it sent me hurtling back to that day in the hospital just after my baby was born, when I was told that I was going to have social services visit me. I don't want to feel that ever again...so I said nothing.

Racism in medical history

The long history of Black distrust of modern medicine is well documented and well founded, a legacy of decades of Black bodies being experimented on without our consent, and racial stereotypes negatively affecting diagnosis and treatment of Black patients.

The legendary British retired psychiatrist and academic, Dr Aggrey Burke shared in an interview with Kehinde Andrews that up until the '1960s, psychosis and conditions such as schizophrenia were seen as affecting highly intelligent, artistic white people, whose creative minds had led them to lose touch with reality. But, when the civil rights era brought Black anger and protest on the streets, psychosis became associated with violence and danger and became a label disproportionately placed on Black bodies.' Burke also believed that 'the reason so many Black people are sectioned is because fear of the violent, disordered, rebellious Black body remains rooted in psychiatric practice'.[9]

As a Black mother, when I admitted that I may have PND, anxiety or any other mental health challenges associated with motherhood, my greatest worry was that services would subconsciously – or consciously – associate my state with cruelty, incompetence and being shambolic. I worried that they would not look at me with the compassion, sympathy and understanding I believed a white mother was more likely to receive.

The history of biases in diagnosis has contributed to my thoughts around this. And across the pond, this has been reiterated. I heard one account with a sickening feeling of familiarity. It was about a young woman who had presented at a gynae clinic complaining of discomfort from her IUD. The doctor was getting ready to remove it. She was not planning to fit another one.

'But why isn't she having another one?' the nurse asked.

'Because she's only going to get pregnant and these devices are expensive; it's just not worth her having another one,' the doctor said, with no idea at all that what she was saying was discriminatory.

Stories like this appal me. That young woman, whom the doctor was dismissing so callously, could easily have been me, typecast and written off, because of my colour. In fact, it has been me, and many other Black women I have spoken to.

I remember reading about the Tuskegee Syphilis Study in the USA where hundreds of Black men from 1932 right up until 1972 were told they were receiving treatment for 'bad blood'.[10] Wait, before you say that this example is not even relevant, in fact, the group consisted of men diagnosed with syphilis, a sexually transmitted disease which, if left untreated, can lead to things like loss of vision and hearing and nerve damage, and a control group of men without the disease. The men with syphilis were not given any treatment and instead they were monitored because the government wanted to know how syphilis would progress if it was left untreated. Inhumane. I was so shocked when I first heard this story, shocked to the core. What happened to the famous first line of the Hippocratic oath? 'First do no harm' – or maybe that should be 'First do no harm to a white person'. Sadly, I now know that this story was far from a one-off.

James Marion Sims was a physician who was practising in the

mid-1800s. His claim to fame was performing experimental vaginal surgery on Black women slaves without giving them any form of pain medication, while they were naked and on their hands and knees.[11] My heart aches and I can almost feel the pain of these poor women, who I feel so connected to, who were degraded and brutalized. The agonizing truth of it, which is almost as hard to take, is the fact that we have these poor unnamed women to thank for 'advances' in vaginal surgeries and, in particular, repair of obstetric fistula. You might think that these things are horrible but mercifully consigned to the history books. Well, you would be mistaken.

In recent history, I found out that, in the USA, so that the public spend could be reduced for Black people, LARC (long-acting reversible contraception) was promoted, mainly with scant regard for any side effects or complications that might arise.[12]

Another experimental device was the Dalkon Shield, implanted into the uterus. It was taken off the market when it was found that it led to life-threatening infections in the poor Black women on whom it was tested and who had it fitted in the early 1970s, as well as embedding itself into the womb. In the 1990s, another LARC device, Norplant – a six-rod device – was implanted into the upper arm of patients to prevent pregnancy, and, yes, it was promoted to poor, Black, often teenage women, seemingly despite the fact that it was known to cause heavy bleeding and headaches as well as weight gain in those women who had it fitted.[13]

All this was done in the name of alleviating poverty, but not poverty in all sectors of society: poverty, and by inference, reproduction, in the Black population. I'm shaking my head as I write this, in disgust, fear and pain. Is there any wonder, I ask myself, that Black women feel very nervous and distrustful of health services that have done them so much harm in history?

The final kick in the teeth came when I read a recent American study that revealed that half of white medical trainees believed, falsely, that Black patients did not 'feel' pain as acutely as white people and had thicker skin than patients who were white.[14]

As a mother, my children are my world. I would literally lay down my life for them – so imagine my horror when I discovered that racial disparities exist in paediatric mental health among Black children, including being less likely to receive pain medication than their white peers.[15] This evidence comes from US studies as there is a lack of information from paediatric mental health services in the UK. The disturbance still hits hard: the thought that either of my girls could be overlooked for or not given pain medication when they needed it, or might be more likely to receive fewer and poorer quality health services than their white peers – that hurt; it hurt a lot.

It seems that the dehumanization of Black women's existence seeps down to Black children, which breaks my heart. I'll stop there, as pain has quickly turned into anger as I write about this nonsensical behaviour – because that's exactly what this is: nonsense.

We are categorized and put in one box

Eden. It means 'place of pleasure and delight'.
This is what we have called our third child.
It's just me and him right now,
Everyone else is asleep,
And although I'm currently sleep deprived...
I wouldn't trade this moment for the world.
He's currently cuddled up to me,
Breastfeeding – and he looks so cozy.

He looks so peaceful,
And I feel like I'm his place of safety.
What a beautiful feeling.

He truly is my place of pleasure and delight,
My place of pleasure and delight.

All three of our children are. But he is our rainbow baby, as we sadly had two consecutive miscarriages within 6 months, shortly before we had him. I couldn't understand why it had to happen to me, to us. I had so many questions but today I'm grateful for Eden, his brother, his sister, and the gift of being a mother. Yes, it truly is a gift.

I can't help but reminisce on the days I had doubts that I could even conceive and fast forward to five years later, I'm a mother of three children aged four and under. Who would have thought?

Our firstborn is Nehemie, which means 'comforted by God'. God comforted us after what seemed like endless years of trying to conceive. Years filled with tears and fear but also hope and faith.

Nehemie is the one who introduced me to motherhood and unconditional love, to lifelong mum friends, to a strength and skills I never thought I possessed, to playgroups where I often felt unwelcome due to being the only Black woman in the room, where I felt no one wanted to engage with me but playgroups where I continued to go for my son's well-being, and to many other beautiful things.

Joëlla which means 'the Lord is God', is our second-born, our one and only daughter, and beautiful sassy princess. She taught me that children can be of the same parent yet be so different in looks and personality. Like her brothers, she makes me experience the highs and lows of motherhood but even after a hard day the highs always outweigh the lows.

Eden is a month old today and although I dreaded transitioning from two to three children, I feel like it is not as bad as I thought it would be and I am learning to not be too hard on myself.

One thing I dread now is the day I will have to explain to my children that there will come a day where they will be made to feel less than because of the colour of their skin. A day where they will be reminded that although they are British, they are Black.

Just like I felt not long ago during Eden's labour.

I had previously heard that Black women are four times more likely to die in childbirth, and I feared that it could happen to me. I feared that I could be next. During my labour, I felt neglected and like what I was saying wasn't taken into consideration while I was agonizing in pain.

After I had Eden, it was later explained to me that he was lying back to back, in a posterior position, which explains why the contraction pains were so unbearable.

After this experience, I could not help but wonder if my treatment had anything to do with the colour of my skin and why us Black women are more likely to die during childbirth. Could neglect and lack of consideration be one of the causes? If another midwife didn't take over, what would have happened to me? How will I begin this conversation with my children?

Sadly, today I was made to feel uncomfortable because I am a Black woman of African heritage. Registering Eden's birth, I was told very confidently that Africa is a country. The staff member seemed surprised and confused when I told them that it was a continent and not a country. I was likewise shocked and confused that in 2022, professionals still won't educate themselves on who we truly are. Although this person may have been innocent, I could not help but feel like we are categorized and put in one box – whether it is done consciously or unconsciously.

I guess with time I'll figure out how to begin this conversation but for now, I'll continue to enjoy my children being sweet, innocent, beautiful souls, and most of all my places of pleasure and delight.

– Judie Ore

Trust betrayed

It was little wonder that I couldn't share how I was feeling after the negative experience I had with my midwife. I had been put in her charge, wide-eyed and clueless, and I was ready to rely on her heavily to guide me through my pregnancy, reassure me when needed, encourage me, answer my questions and generally be my cheerleader. And although I had a few friends who almost idolized their midwives, and credited them with giving them the reassurance and the help they needed and which had made their pregnancy and eventual birth of their babies the wonderful experience that it should be, my midwife had betrayed me in the worst way possible. Sometimes I shudder to think what would have happened if the social worker, who recognized so easily what was going on, had not been Black or had been of the same bigoted stock as my midwife.

But this is what inadequate recognition of our mental health needs leads to: an imbalance of power and authority between Black mothers and providers. Cultural naivety in services can no longer be justified, nor can being insensitive and discriminating towards the needs of Black women. This adds to our negative experiences. It is a sad litany and it seems to me that not much has changed since women knelt naked before surgeons who thought it was fine to experiment on them and cut their most sensitive and private parts with no pain relief at all.

I know that during the Coronavirus pandemic, love for the NHS was at an all-time high, but that does not mean that it isn't racist, not by any means. I can't stress this enough. A staggering 60% of Black people in the UK do not believe that their health is as equally protected or valued as a white person's.[16] I co-sign this. That is a high percentage and an awful lot of people who do not have faith in the medical care they are entitled to.

From what I have experienced first-hand and from my research, it seems to me indisputable that the Black community is more at risk in the medical system than their white counterparts due to both medical ignorance and an unconscious bias.

Racism has been institutionalized so much that I often believe people don't even recognize how serious it is. In the UK, Black women are four times more likely to die in childbirth than white women.[17] When I spoke about these statistics and the explicit stories behind them on BBC News and other national broadcasting channels, someone sent to me a triggering tweet saying that 'racism must sound like a better excuse than pre-existing health problems aye'. Black people are not the only people with pre-existing health conditions! This is an example of the constant gaslighting Black women feel, as if the systemic oppression we face daily in every area of life is non-existent or trivial. The irony is that so many people believe racism and systemic oppression against Black people ended in the 1960s. If it wasn't so harmful, it would be laughable.

I discovered that the people participating in studies about trusting health professionals reiterated that trust was only gained with the interpersonal and technical competence of physicians.[18] In one report on African Americans' views, additional factors contributing to distrust were 'a perception that they were elitist, expectations of racism and the suspicion that there might be experimentation during routine provision of healthcare. Trust appears to facilitate care-seeking behaviour and promotes patient honesty and adherence'.[19] Patient adherence describes the extent to which an individual's behaviour positively corresponds to the health-related recommendations and advice of that individual's healthcare provider or healthcare professional.[20] Distrust will put us off seeking help or advice. Quite often, this will lead to us changing doctors or it might mean that we do not follow medical advice.

If you look more closely, you will find that there are always unique factors that make for distrust, especially in the studies that have been carried out where many Black patients say that they do not feel certain that their doctors will always act in their best interest. And I can certainly relate to that perception. What happened to me is a very good example.

I have to reiterate, I had *never* encountered social services until the day I gave birth to my first daughter, and then the reason I did encounter them was the racial bias and prejudice of a midwife. That experience led me to believe that she and the rest of the healthcare services could not be trusted. It is truly horrible to feel the weight of the establishment bearing down on you and knowing that if they want to, they can take your child. We have all heard the horror stories of families having children taken into care erroneously and having to fight to get them back. Of course, there are instances when the removal of children is entirely warranted, and I do know that social workers have a very hard job to do – damned if they do and damned if they don't – but my experience was truly terrifying.

I was a new mother wondering if my baby was going to be taken away and feeling hopeless and helpless under the scrutiny.

Lack of trust doesn't come from nowhere

The statistics that surround Black mothers not accessing perinatal care cannot be adequately addressed without first understanding and then dismantling racism and bias in the healthcare system. The lack of trust doesn't come from nowhere. And as I shared my own story with a wider audience, my network, newspapers, mainstream news, both television and radio and online, I found my own experience and similar stories resonated with many other women. Just like me, many of them chose to struggle on their own rather than seek care.

My experience was that my words were carelessly and recklessly taken out of context, for me to be judged, shown no empathy, and then exposed to the risk having my family torn apart.

Inequality

I feel safest in the hands of Black doctors

Forty hours into my induction of my twin daughters, I was only 4cm dilated. Throughout my pregnancy I had resisted all suggestions of a planned caesarean from my doctors, but now my husband and I resignedly began to discuss this eventuality as labour didn't seem to be progressing. So, we eventually relented and asked to discuss an elected caesarean.

I'll never forget how the white consultant on duty tersely told me that I should have opted for an elected caesarean weeks before, as he had advised. He made me feel as though I had wasted everyone's time, as though labouring in the way I wanted to, to birth my children, wasn't really my decision. I remember asking him about the chances of a caesarean if I continued with the induction and he informed me that something like 1 in 2 women have an emergency caesarean after induction so 'either way, you'll likely end up on the table'.

I remember feeling deeply upset by his crass words, his insensitivity, his rudeness. I couldn't believe that I was being chastised like this when at my most vulnerable.

My planned caesarean was escalated to an emergency after doctors could not detect a heartbeat for my younger twin, and during the surgery I lost around three times the usual amount of blood. I thought we were all doing well, but a few days later, I suddenly felt faint and breathless. Doctors established that my haemoglobin levels were low because of the blood loss. I was told that my blood work was normal immediately following the surgery, but I remember thinking: If my doctors knew I had lost more blood than usual, then why had my iron levels not been more closely monitored? Had medics assumed I would be OK because I'm Black, and therefore stronger than a white woman?

In the following weeks and months, as the world went into lockdown, I pushed down any difficult memories of my hospital experience. I do consider that I was generally well cared for, but I cannot deny that there were moments of real dissatisfaction with my care, moments that are traumatizing and deeply upsetting to relive.

Fifteen months on, I've developed a sense of wariness towards doctors treating my family and me, because I cannot trust that they will treat us with the sensitivity and care that we deserve. I sometimes delay seeking treatment or asking for help because I am reluctant to expose myself to potential insensitivity at the very least, or danger at the very worst, from my healthcare providers. Where I am able to choose my doctors, I generally pick a Black doctor where possible and that is because of what I perceive as their ability to cross the empathy barrier and truly connect with me as their patient.

I feel safest in the hands of Black doctors.

During my pregnancy, I saw a number of midwives and specialist obstetricians, but my experiences with a kindly Black midwife and a Black obstetrician were the best. They were both warm and kind, and I received more from them than bland, sympathetic professionalism. They seemed to genuinely care for my wellbeing. Their smiles reached their eyes, their voices conveyed an honest warmth – not a thinly veiled impatience. I will forever be indebted to the African midwives who looked after me while I recovered from my long labour and C-section. Those wonderful women quietly taught me how to nurse my children and gently insisted that I feed my babies formula when waiting for my milk to come in, so that we all safely got through those first few days.

What many of us might feel in our bones is supported by empirical data, where we see that Black men receive better care at the hands of Black medics,[21] Black neonates are more likely to survive when cared for by Black doctors[22] and Black people experience less anxiety and pain when treated by Black doctors.[23]

So, while we often see the mistrust Black people have of the medical community attributed to cultural factors, it is more than that – it is grounded in factual, life-and-death experiences.

And we all just want to live another day.

– Zara Oteng

Structural racism and Black women failing to access care has had a massive impact on my journey. A system where public policies, institutional practices and cultural representations work to reinforce and perpetuate racial inequity in obstetrics and gynaecology is putting Black women and their children at risk. So, what is the answer?

If anyone claims institutional racism doesn't exist, how do we explain noticeable gaps at all levels? The lack of representation of Black women in senior positions is undeniable, so I would think that denying institutional racism *is* racist in itself.

As I see it, by increasing representation in senior positions, Black women may feel more encouraged to gain real trust in healthcare services. The lack of representation and visibility of Black women in senior positions is daunting and scary – not only do I feel unseen, I cannot see myself in those who are in a position to make real change. The worst part is there hasn't been much of a shift in the proportion of Black appointments to Trust boards or senior leadership positions within the healthcare sector. If that sounds discouraging, imagine also knowing that Black staff are twice as likely to enter the disciplinary process and expect to wait 50 per cent longer than white colleagues for a promotion.[24]

'We have to hire those that are suitable for such positions.' I can imagine this being said to justify the under-representation. Pushing the blame on Black people for lack of attainment in an intensely racist world – triggering. It implies that this elephant in the room boils down to our biological differences and that our societal structures do not discriminate.

The Motherhood Group was commissioned by NHS England and NHS Improvement to investigate Black and ethnic minority mothers' experiences of accessing perinatal mental health services, and the barriers they have encountered. I held four workshops speaking directly with mums and they shared their thoughts on so many themes. One of the recommendations I have proposed, based on what all of the mums in the workshop said, is the need to improve and make clear the process for complaints in NHS maternity and perinatal mental health services. The mothers also felt that more Black women should be involved in leadership positions to ensure accountability and cultural diversity at all stages of service provision. This feedback echoes my sentiments, confirming that there is a heavy desire for more staff who look like us – Black women. Although not all mums in the workshop felt like they had received perfect, attentive or personalized care from every single staff member who did look like them during their antenatal or perinatal period, they often felt that Black staff might be able to better understand the context of their concerns.

The NHS Workforce Race Equality Standard aims to improve BAME representation at senior management and board level, but what exactly is BAME representation? The term BAME is lazy and weak. It clumps us all together and is not 'inclusive', especially since we can't ignore how anti-Blackness is so rife. 'Non-whites' are not all the same, especially when it comes to health outcomes.

One thing that has struck me is the fact that despite this or that committee and endless think tanks and task forces and research, there remains a woeful lack of accountability. There is still, of course, the fallback position of typecasting Black people to the extent that there is no doubt that sometimes and, in some situations, we have almost been conditioned to 'know our place'. Call me the stereotypical Black woman who speaks up and is seen as angry, aggressive and a bully. That's happened to me in literally every single establishment and industry I've entered. Society tells us that Black women are just reverting to this stereotype if we dare to speak up for ourselves. I know the feeling and maybe without even consciously thinking about it, there would be times when I know I would not be as comfortable as a white woman to advocate for myself. I wanted to share some stories of Black people working within the NHS to give you an idea of what it is really like.

Stories from the front

Morvia Gooden, former nurse and senior programme lead at the NHS Leadership Academy, has written a really interesting article in which she says:

> I began my career at the age of 18. I worked hard, passed all my exams and gained the relevant qualifications to become a nurse. At that time, there were two levels of nursing – a State Enrolled Nurse (SEN) and a State Registered Nurse (SRN). Within this two-tier system an SRN was at a higher level than an SEN and I had all the qualifications to be working at the higher level. However, after applying to become a nurse, during my interview I was asked if I would prefer to be a SEN nurse, which was the lower-level role. Being a naive teenager, I didn't think anything of it, but fortunately for me my mother worked as an auxiliary nurse and advised me not to accept the lower-level role. Once I began my career as an SRN, I saw many black nurses working as SENs, which was sad to see. My experiences as a nurse continued to show discrimination against black women in the NHS. In 1988 I applied and successfully became a midwife. It was at a time when black midwives were brought in to support and help build up the NHS; however, the treatment they received was shockingly poor. I remember one

of the white sisters on the ward warning me about what happened to black midwives: 'They bring you in as a black midwife to boost their numbers but once you're in, they will discard you.' Over the coming weeks and months I saw a lot of this taking place as one by one each black midwife was out of a job. In the 21st century you'd hope that individual behaviours would change but yet we're still working in a health system where:

- Last year, 75% of acute trusts reported a large number of black, Asian and minority ethnic (BAME) staff being bullied. According to the NHS Workforce and Race Equality Standard, 41% of BAME colleagues said that they were being bullied, harassed or abused compared with 18% of white staff in similar roles
- The under-representation of BAME colleagues is still continuing. The Snowy White Peaks report highlighted that in London, a city where 40% of the workforce and patients are BAME, 17 out of 40 trusts had all white boards.[25]

I was touched by what Morvia had to say. Despite her obvious love for what she did and her devotion to her patients, she had been frustrated with elements of her job.

'A long way to go' probably sums up the picture pretty well and I can certainly add my own experience to that of Morvia, because although I was not on the staff, I still felt that I was the lowest priority and had to almost apologize for being there. Indeed, I was sent away twice before I was finally allowed to stay and have my baby, and that felt terrible. I had put myself in their hands, I was terrified and wildly excited to meet my baby Zoe all at the same time, and I knew it was not going to be easy. I told myself I would be with comforting and knowledgeable midwives who would guide me through the miracle of birth.

What I did not expect was to have to beg for attention and to feel as though I was getting in the way. I was not surprised when, after reading Morvia's article, I read that a survey of NHS staff from non-white ethnic groups had shown that almost 15.5% of them reported being discriminated against either by another colleague, a team leader or a manager in the preceding 12 months, a figure that was over double of the number of white staff who reported similar issues.[26]

Unequal career progression opportunities

When I think about my experience in the NHS, it makes sense to look at what is going on within an organization because that will affect how the people in that organization operate in the wider community. I was particularly interested in what Morvia had to say about her having to fight tooth and nail to progress in her career and to break into what looked very much like the preserve of white staff members within her specialism of neurology.

Sadly, in my experience, Black women are often thought of as being incompetent, lazy and unwilling to work, which isn't the case at all. It makes me feel as though I'm ten steps behind everyone else, trying to catch up with something that I'll never be able to reach. I feel as though I can't be accepted for who I am because of the division in society which dictates that white men in power is the norm. Anything other than this doesn't fit the stereotype and therefore isn't accepted. If you look at the people at the helm of an organization, you'll see that a majority, if not all, are white men, while those at the bottom of the hierarchy are from under-represented groups. This didn't just happen incidentally; it's human nature to aspire to be in the company of people who are similar to you and something that is commonly referred to as the mini-me syndrome. Those working at board level may dispute this, but it's very much the case in my experience. For example, I've sat at a board meeting and put forward an idea or suggestion to not much response or buy-in, but then a few minutes later, a man has presented a similar idea and been applauded and recognized for his efforts. It may not seem much, but over time these micro inequities build up and you start to internalize these subtle forms of oppression. The net result is that you feel smaller and ultimately not valued.

As a system, what are we going to do about inequality?

The NHS Workforce Race Equality Standard study in 2019 showed that 69.9% of ethnic minority staff believed that the NHS trust they work for provides equal opportunities for career progression or promotion, compared with 86.3% of white staff.[27]

And I'm pretty sure that 69.9% of the 'ethnic minority' would not fully represent Black people accurately.

Reading about Morvia's work was an eye-opener and gave me a good insight into what is happening at the heart of the NHS. From this, I believe there is a connection between the experience of racism towards staff in the NHS and the experiences of Black mothers. Many women will most certainly play both roles, and the challenges they face to be treated fairly and equally will be exacerbated as a result. Surely being on the receiving end of racism as a healthcare professional could indeed put a strain on your mental health, which potentially could negatively affect the way Black mothers are supported and treated by those that look like them the most.

Black motherhood adds another layer of depth

Motherhood to me is the most rewarding and yet exhausting job I'll ever experience. It's filled with dizzy highs and worrying lows but it's something that I've been blessed to experience and I wouldn't change it for the world.

Black motherhood adds another layer of depth, as although I have an unshakeable commitment to continuing the excellence present in my DNA, I can't help but feel fear at the world because my sisters are suffering at an alarming rate when we think about maternal care.

Prior to giving birth, I was aware that Black women were disproportionately mistreated in our healthcare system and I'll be honest, this was always something that lingered in the back of my mind. I even requested for my 'White' best friend to be my second birthing partner just in case my voice was drowned out or my concerns weren't heard. However, reflecting back, this was far from what I had experienced. I actually had positive maternal care throughout my pregnancy, labour and aftercare. I was considered high risk because of my fibroids and felt healthcare professionals listened to my needs and concerns. Was this because the majority of the professionals I came in contact with were from BME backgrounds or was it because I had my NHS badge with me? Is my experience likely to be similar now that I live in a less diverse area? These are thoughts that go through my mind regularly.

I remember when I found out I was pregnant and I was elated. However, this quickly disappeared because I didn't have an easy pregnancy. I was diagnosed with hyperemesis gravidarum at six weeks, which lasted until I gave birth. I had gone from feelings of joy and euphoria to depression. I remember asking myself whether I could possibly continue with the pregnancy; a topic so taboo which challenged my Christian values and faith. It wasn't my lack of trust in the healthcare system that stopped me from asking for help, it was my culture and this notion of what it means to be a Strong Black Woman – a statement which is more detrimental than celebratory.

My family ingrained a deep sense of independence into me, which is part and parcel of being not only a woman but a Black Ghanaian woman at that. Being surrounded by strong Black mothers definitely empowered me but also made me feel that asking for help would show signs of weakness. When I eventually struck up the courage to speak to loved ones, it wasn't welcomed with open arms and it reinforced my decision to internalize my thoughts and suffer in silence. They couldn't understand the depths of my depression and I couldn't adequately explain the help I needed and desired. My family is deeply rooted in Christianity and so the response I tended to receive was to pray about things becoming better and to have faith, but when I had thoughts on whether I wanted to continue with the pregnancy, how could I possibly pray when it contradicted everything I was feeling?

I felt myself resenting being pregnant, then the baby arrived and all that changed. I was met with an indescribable love but once again no one talked about the difficulties of motherhood in the first four months. From sleepless nights to troubles breast-feeding, there was a constant worry that I wasn't doing everything right and it gnawed at me. I felt so low and I was struggling, and although family were there for me physically, they lacked in giving me the emotional support I needed. I vividly remember a family member telling me not to cry too much, otherwise I would end up with postnatal depression. Once again, the prospects of having a mental health issue were brushed under the carpet and I was forced to deal with it internally. I spoke to my health visitor who was supportive and encouraged me to seek psychological support, but I refused because I didn't want to be perceived as incapable. Depression is talked about a lot but no one really speaks about OCD – intrusive thoughts of harm coming towards your baby. Though I knew I would never act on these thoughts, and coming from a psychological background, I was well aware of what was happening and they were just thoughts, how could I speak about them when I was just expected to get over it? I found it incredibly difficult to try and verbalize my thoughts, when people just assumed my experiences were just the troubles that came with being a mum.

To improve my mental health I decided to attend baby groups, which helped rid me of the feelings of isolation. I joined The Motherhood Group and it was lovely hearing stories from women who looked like me; it normalized that it was okay not being okay. I felt a sense of community and it is something that I will forever hold dearly.

My daughter is everything to me. I look at her and I imagine all of the great things I want her to accomplish, but I am grounded when I consider the obstacles I have faced and that she is likely to in the future unless significant change is made.

– *Stephanie deGraft-Johnson*

I, like many others, probably thought that Barack Obama would bring about some sort of epiphany many years ago with his success as President of the USA and arguably leader of the Western world. In office between 2009 and 2017, he made people see things differently and you could be forgiven for feeling that, at last, things were going to change. Fast-forward three years and we have the tragic death of George Floyd, a Black man who died after a white officer kneeled on his neck despite his pleas that he could not breathe. That was followed by the protests in the UK where statues of figures associated with the slave trade were torn down, and rightly so.

Then in the week when the police officer responsible for the death of George Floyd was convicted on all counts, another young Black boy was shot dead by a white policewoman who apparently mistook her gun for her taser.[28]

It seems that the struggle will be ongoing. I am passionate about the area of Black equality surrounding women and their experiences having babies in the UK, but I am always conscious of the struggles, great and small, that go on every day, all over the world.

A short poem I wrote about Zoe and Chloe sums up my recent thoughts.

My Black daughters

Often I think about my daughters, my Black daughters,
As they grow up into womanhood – and the experiences they
*   might have when and if they decide to become mothers*
*   themselves one day.*
Will they have a positive experience when interacting with
*   maternity care – healthcare as a whole?*
If I'm being honest, sometimes it makes me feel a little anxious,
To possibly imagine them in a similar situation to what I and
*   many other Black women have gone through when trying to*
*   access adequate care.*
But somewhere, deep down, I do have a glimpse of hope...
Hope that they will feel safe,
Positive,
Have confidence,
And will trust the healthcare system – at least more than our
*   generation does.*

– Sandra Igwe

Does lack of trust in the healthcare system stop me from asking for help?

My short response to this would be no. However, the journey of getting to this mindset has come from me having to deal with many incidents where my concerns and those around me, that are also Black, were not regarded in the light that they should have initially been.

I remember whilst deep in labour I had asked for the epidural, as the pain was way too much for me to physically handle any more. I cried, pleaded, screamed and more. I kept getting told that the person to administer the epidural would be here soon, that they were caught up in another room. Some time would go by, more screaming, crying and pleading, and I would be told the same thing. A few more moments would pass and again, the same thing: they will be here soon. Until it got to a point where my daughter was no longer wanting to remain in limbo, and she arrived.

After hearing her first cry, I was so relieved. Everything else did not matter any more. She was here, she was safe, I was here, I was safe. No more contractions. No more inhaling gas and air as though nothing else in this world exists. No more having to restrain myself from the urge to push because the midwife can see what I cannot. No more. However, when everything had settled down, I was later informed that they had not called for the epidural that I was screaming down the hospital for, because I looked as though I could handle the pain.

Yes, that is right, I was denied what I had requested due to looking like I could handle labour (whatever that means). Despite my screaming, crying, pleading and experiencing one of the worst pains there is to feel and experience as a human being, I was told that I looked strong enough to endure it. Even though there is literally the option to not by being given the epidural.

However, I must admit, at the time I was slightly relieved to hear this due to the complications I had heard some women experience after receiving an epidural (such as continuous back pain, headaches, loss of bladder control, to name a few). But at the same time, I had not even deeply comprehended that my cry for help was dismissed based upon how I looked. What more would I have needed to have done to show that I truly needed what I was asking for? Did I need to go on my knees and continue crying there? Oh, I forgot, I had done that too, but I guess a pregnant woman on her knees whilst in labour begging for stronger pain relief looks strong enough to continue enduring the pain of childbirth.

When you are in such a vulnerable situation, you want to be

able to trust that whoever has been assigned to you has your and your child's best interests at the forefront of every decision that is being medically made. Regardless of race, class, religion or educational background, the woman in labour should have full faith that her needs, requests and concerns are considered in the same light as anyone else's.

Fast-forward roughly six years after giving birth to my daughter, and the realization that this was not the case came to light when I was sharing my birthing story with a good friend of mine who is French and white. We had spent many moments sharing our experiences in regard to unfairness in the workplace, day-to-day covert racism and everything in between. Comparing how that looks like for us both. However, I did not think that my birthing story was among one of those moments. We were just two single mothers talking about our experiences.

As I came to tell her about the part of my labour experience where I was told they had purposely not given me the epidural, she paused and proceeded to say, 'Yvonne, this is not right! This goes against your human rights!' And just like that, a story I had told many times over had changed. At no point had I even considered my human rights, I was just relieved to be able to tell the story of how my daughter arrived as I know many Black women have not been able to due to the lack of regard to them and their baby.

Now, if we go back to my initial answer of me not being held back in asking for help despite my lack of trust in the healthcare system, you can see that it never even made a difference. I still asked, many times over, and I was not heard. I screamed, pleaded and cried, and was still not listened to. My request was overshadowed by me looking strong enough. On the hospital floor. Begging for pain relief. Looking strong enough.

My lack of trust in the healthcare system does not stop me from asking for help; however, it stops me from believing that every decision being made is being filtered purely through the lens of professionalism. I understand we are human and by human nature we learn to make certain biases and assumptions based upon our own understanding of the world. But if there is one place that a woman should be able to tell you she is in pain and she should be listened to based upon her knowing herself and her pain threshold, it is in the labour room.

I thank God that nothing detrimental came about as a result of my labour experience; however, many Black women cannot say the same thing. And that is the scary part. That even at a time when we have so many medical advancements, it seems as though the thinking of some professionals has remained stuck in a time that is no more.

There are moments when, due to being a Black mother, I suddenly find myself in situations such as being denied an epidural because I look as though I can handle the pain I am in (despite literally screaming that I cannot and despite the fact that labour is literally one of THE most painful experiences a person can go through). Or going on holiday and having to be on guard for anyone wanting to film or take pictures of me and my child (without asking), purely due to our being Black. I know for the most part, a non-Black mother might read this with disbelief, confusion and probably a sense of relief that as a non-Black mother she does not have to deal with and experience. But empathy would not be possible.

So, having said all of this, what does Black motherhood mean to me? It means that at times my child and I are going to go through some situations that can only be understood by some. It means that I must be ready to have mini battles for basic human rights. It means that I have to consider our race in scenarios where race should not ever be a factor. It means that my walk and journey in motherhood will be scrutinized differently and at times unjustly in comparison to some of my peers. It means that I must make sure that I keep myself surrounded by those who fully understand the silent pains. It means that regardless of all of this and more, I would do it all over again just to make sure my child (and future children) will not have to go through certain things that I went through. It means that I am willing to do what a mother would for their child/children; it just so happens that I was born Black.

– *Yvonne Ihegborow*

Normalize Black mums sharing their thoughts, feelings and emotions

Black motherhood and mental health

Another day here we go, get daughter ready for nursery, dropped off check, drive to work in rush hour, check in on mum, is she safe, has carer turned up, what frame of mind is she in, check in on her during the day – heart pounding as carer leaves, I get through the work day, rush back up to pick daughter up from nursery, clock watching the whole way as timing is tight + traffic is building, reach with couple minutes to spare, can finally breathe. Rush back to do work admin/calls, give daughter quick snack then back down to mum's to make her dinner, check she is okay. Bedtime looming so rush to make sure mum is settled, get daughter ready to head back home to bedtime. Body shattered, brain frazzled, patience reducing, tiredness kicking in but know I have to continue, bedtime routine (brush teeth, wash, PJs on, read story). Now 10pm and can finally have me time for the day. This daily struggle/jiggle is so hard, overwhelming and at times deflating. When can I find time for me, for self-care, who can I talk to that will understand my daily struggles, feelings? Everyone tells me you're doing a great job, your mum will be so proud of you, your daughter is a representation of your hard work. For me it's just another day of juggling along and hoping to get through the day.

– Senitta

Mothers are usually led to put their children first and this often leads to them neglecting their mental health. We are usually expected to be strong and hold a brave face 'for the sake of the children', which is what usually leads to poor mental health. Mothers should embrace every bit of themselves, the good, the bad and the ugly. Holding feelings in does more harm than good. It is okay to cry, it is okay to get it wrong, it is okay not to know what to do, it is okay to feel sad, it is okay to get angry.

Women should feel free to be and express themselves as they please, whether they have children or not. It is also okay to put yourself first because this leads to better mental state.

– Shelley

I felt very low after giving birth to my second daughter, I struggled with trying to deal with my mental health and being a mother of two children. When reaching out to my family I was made to feel that I was making a fuss over nothing. One family member stated, 'That's not your portion, imagine what women back home deal with, you are fine.' I felt unsupported, alone and the need to get on with it.

I was made to feel unable to share how I was feeling emotionally because as a Black woman we always need to appear strong and be everyone else's support system, but who is supporting us?

– Emmanuela Eqyavoen

Ever since I was a child, I have always felt the need to be strong, dominant and avoid showing weakness at all costs. Crying was a weakness, showing emotion was something to be laughed at, telling my mother how I felt would surely result in ridicule.

And so as I became an adult, I had no idea how to explore my emotions and manage them in friendships and relationships. I was unaware that I could reach out for help, and as my 30s approached, my mental health began to deteriorate unexpectedly and dramatically.

During my pregnancy, I sought the help and advice of a Black midwife. For the first time, I felt comfortable to confide in someone who looked like me. I truly felt as if the generational curse of keeping things in and not bothering anyone had slightly lifted. Today I am happy. I attend therapy, talk to my partner instead of dwindling down and push myself to open up.

– Tameka Braun

There is a lack of support for Black women in regard to their mental health. There is a stigma when Black women even talk about mental health. As an African, mental health is disregarded. This has a domino effect on generation upon generation as Black women internalize their feelings. This is not only with family but with health practitioners. Black women in addition do not have as many resources as other races – there may be BAME resources but this is not targeted to Black women specifically. Most especially mothers from African backgrounds.

– Angela and Victoria

No one ever prepares you for the mental challenges of motherhood, especially becoming a first-time mother. But I am grateful for being true and honest about how I felt and also accepting help and support from my partner, family and friends.

– Amuda

Black motherhood and mental health has always been a topic that is dear to my heart. Being a Black mother and experiencing amounts of anxiety and depression in my son's early years really affected the way I parented.

At times I was unable to be there for my son in the capacity I wish I was able to be, due to being in a low mood, wanting to sleep excessively and overthinking.

That's why I think as a Black woman and, most importantly, a Black mother, it's important to talk about these issues that are normally seen as a taboo in our community.

Having events like this to be vulnerable without judgement, seeking therapy, communicating with your family network and them knowing ways they can support you without you feeling like you're a burden.

I want to thank The Motherhood Group for holding events like this that enable us as Black mothers to be comfortable in discussing these issues.

– Hilary Speaks

If it wasn't for social media and finding pages like The Motherhood Group, etc., I feel like I wouldn't know where to find support for my mental health, other than sometimes having the support from my family and friends. There is no real help for your mental state after having a child, especially with this pandemic when it's needed the most. Good, free counselling is very hard to come by unless you are on the verge of self-harming or harming others around you. I also feel like the people that would be allocated to us as Black women for our mental health are hardly ever Black women or even women of colour. We need more people that can relate to us as Black women in the position to help our people. It's hard trying to open up to someone who cannot relate in any way.

– Shartay Eduh

Being Black comes with its struggles, being a woman comes with struggles and being a mother comes with its struggles. So imagine being all three.

Sometimes in my life, I feel like having to mentally multitask will take a serious toll on your mental health and your social life, because not only do you have to focus on being a mum, and the best you can be, you have to think about being a woman trying to work, trying to stay healthy mentally and physically for your children and trying to maintain a social life and in some ways keeping everyone happy.

I don't do it anymore. I will no longer try to keep EVERYONE happy. It's not my responsibility; my responsibility is my children. I'm determined to be in the right space mentally and physically to raise the best human beings possible.

– Melina Adewade

We don't need to be strong. We need to be aware of our feelings and emotions. We need to reach out and speak to each other because we might be surprised at the fact that we are not the only ones that feel a certain way or have been through a particular experience. Good mental health is something we all need and must aspire to achieve.

– Keera

Black mothers are not afforded the same compassion and care when it comes to postnatal depression and depression generally. Their parenting is judged and they are forcibly sectioned against their will rather than offered any therapeutic care or counselling. As a result of these fears, a lot of Black mothers refuse to engage with mental health teams due to their racism and anti-Blackness attitude towards Black women and mothers.

I would like to see more support given to new Black mothers before it reaches crisis stage.

More funding for Black counsellors – more Black mothers

prefer to open up to people who have cultural competency, not those who hold negative stereotypes of the Black community. I would like to see professionals not have access to vulnerable Black service users unless they have taken a cultural competency course with certificate and evidence on helping Black women, not locking them in a mental asylum and contributing to losing their kids.

– Zia Teshome

Mental health is REAL. I would have never thought I would experience such a crazy thing. I never knew I would have it. Having my son Temi is amazing. He is beautiful. However, I was crashing and didn't realize. I had my husband's support but it wasn't enough. I was breastfeeding. I would be angry if anyone told me it's not enough. That I should give him formula. I didn't want anyone to help me, I just knew I needed help. My labour experience was tough. And I stopped praying.

However, once I crashed, I realized I do not need help, my mum and husband were always there to support me. They looked after Temi while I slept. I started self-care, which I believe is important – and to stop having mum guilt. I realized once I was looking after myself. I became a better wife and mum. Nothing perfect, but I use the time to make sure I am the best person and wife I can be.

– Chi Chi Odulate

The need...
To know that time out is okay.
To listen to yourself and others.
To know when to ask for help.
To know it's okay to do it tomorrow.
To get everything right.
To be successful.

To know it's okay to take a break.
To be independent.
To find trust.
To be able to receive help.
To be perfect.
To know you can rebuild.

At times I struggle with 'the need' to be perfect. I feel guilty to leave my daughter but I know she will be okay. I struggle with separation anxiety; it's my job to always have her with me, to buy her stuff.

I need to understand that time apart is good for both of us, and she won't feel any type of way being away from mummy.

I need to understand it is okay to ask for help, and I'm not perfect.

Growth comes with time.

– Cassandra Williams

Awareness of self for my child

Primarily I advocate for my child's health. Advocate in times of adversity – in the challenges that come and are won – and are and have to be won again.

For my child, she will have awareness of culture and birthright in creating an identity and sense of self and of belonging.

Being able to stand and withstand alienation and to be standing proud when the storms are around us and after the storm has passed.

Knowledge that the disadvantages that we as women have
and
Being proud of your skin and the skin that you are in

Of your hair and embrace your difference and your hair that grows to the sun.

– Anonymous

CHAPTER 3

When She Can't Be Depressed Because She's Black

Black mothers are expected to bend over backwards for everyone except themselves. They are expected to raise their child, work and sleep minimal hours at the expense of their mental health. They are expected to teach their children, discipline their children, keep a clean home, cook nutritious meals for their children every day at the expense of their mental health. They should do all this with a smile on their face, and God forbid should they complain because they are so, so lucky and blessed to have been able to bring children into the world. They should be happy to give up their career, their social lives and their sanity because the priority is and will always be the child. It shouldn't matter if their child's father is living the exact life he had before becoming a father; we as mothers should not complain because it is our duty to take on the primary parenting role because we alone carried and gave birth to our children – not him. Time and time again we are told repeatedly to neglect ourselves for the sake of others when, in actuality, it should be the complete opposite. We should be taught to put ourselves first above all, because if we do not fill ourselves up, how then shall we pour out and give to our children? How then shall we love, nurture and be present with our children if we are not able to offer these things to ourselves first? To love our children is to love ourselves first – this is the most important lesson of motherhood.

– Liz K

My friend and I shook with laughter at one of our favourite little brunch spots in Shoreditch. I almost knocked over my coffee in hysterics. Our children were with their dads that morning, so it was just the two of us. Finally, some adult time and space for me to be just Sandra.

'They really lied to us about motherhood,' my friend said, giggling, but I noticed a sort of melancholic look in her eyes. 'I mean, would you have agreed to be a mum if you'd known the truth?'

We were both smiling at this point, but she wasn't wrong. I knew precious little about the stress and loneliness of motherhood before I got pregnant. My friend and I went to school together and had wild dreams of becoming corporate professionals. We went on to do further studies after university so that we could make our mark on the world. And why not?

Some women expect motherhood to give them direction and purpose, but – for me, at least, and many women I know – it sometimes turns out to be the opposite. Motherhood threw a large wrench in my plans.

I remember when Zoe was only a few days old. I laid her down for a nap and heaved great sobs alone on the couch. I was lonely, so lonely. *This isn't at all what I thought my life would be as a new mum*, I thought. *What am I doing wrong?* I even decided to go back to work earlier, when she was just five months old, just so that I could get some adult interaction, regain my purpose, feel as though I was doing something other than 'just being a mum'. This was one of the worst mistakes of my life, and I shortly had to reverse my decision to go back to work.

Sitting with my friend in the warm July air, I felt confident that I was finally out of the woods. I liked my life and loved the new version of myself. I looked at my friend and could remember the stage that she was currently in, where I felt lied to, and also felt I had lost my whole self and desperately needed to find my enthusiasm for life again.

I adored our two small daughters. But, Lord, my life would have looked very different if I'd known about the dangers of Black maternal mental health before I got pregnant.

Depression was once described by Winston Churchill as a black dog. Corrina Horne writes:

> The black dog is an effective metaphor because depression can feel like an ominous, long-suffering presence tracking your every move. The black dog of depression represents the gradual overtaking of the things you once loved, the person you once recognized in the mirror, or the life you once lived.[29]

As she puts it, depression does not take annual leave; instead, it can follow you around 'like a shadow – a large, lumbering shadow'.

The feeling of depression as a new mother robs you of all the joy of life – well, so I thought at the time. Even the simple things like enjoying some toast and peanut butter or a walk in the park on a sunny day at the time felt as though they could not offer any joy. I had a new baby and people constantly bounced up to me admiring my beautiful daughter, and at the time, I almost felt that I had to constantly force myself to smile and thank them.

I was expected to be a delighted new mother with bluebirds flying overhead and angels singing and the garden full of roses. I felt deep love for my new daughter and I was achingly proud of her, but I also felt as though my heart was breaking, if only it had the energy to do that. It felt like wading through treacle, and hardly even having the energy to breathe. I went through the motions and did what I had to do, smiled when I knew I should and even attempted a laugh when needed. Underneath all that was an all-encompassing misery that made every day a real effort to live through. I felt a deep sense of loss, a loss of my identity, the Sandra I was before, carefree and somewhat selfish... Anxiety filled me. As I looked at the beautiful child in my arms, I was desperate to be able to enjoy every moment of her.

How Black women are perceived

Woah, just writing that brings a sense of relief, therapeutic almost. Being able to share my honest true feelings, without fear of judgement, shame or being painted with a brush of the stereotypical Black women tropes:

The Angry Black Woman

The Strong Black Woman

The Video Vixen, aka Jezebel Black Woman

Feeling as though every response, action or word uttered automatically puts you within one or all these categories is exhausting. This kind of stereotyping has affected how I'm seen at work, in health establishments and life in general, but the scariest part is that somehow it affected how I saw myself. And the manifestation of the stereotypes has also played its part in the development and the continuation of the anxiety that I felt as a new mother.

And I would be lying if I said there is no shortage of perceived *Strong Black Women* to look towards for examples of women who have led the way: Maya Angelou, Oprah Winfrey and Chimamanda

Ngozi Adichie – who, by the way, I named my younger daughter after: Chloe Chimamanda Igwe. Then every tough and no-nonsense Black grandma, big Mumma or aunty who persisted and persevered and kept us all on the straight and narrow when we were growing up. But the flipside of this is the strong Black woman who, to the detriment of her own mental and physical health, keeps going and does not want to make a fuss. I consider myself one of the latter – well, at least on my early motherhood journey. We don't want to make a fuss, we have been conditioned not to, and we pay for it with our mental health.

The stereotype of the *Angry Black Woman* is the woman who will cut you down with a mouthful of sharp words, or who acts irrationally aggressively but no one thinks that perhaps she is simply passionate or hurt, and her anger is justified due to the ongoing attacks from those who just don't understand. Which in turn leads to high levels of anxiety – at least that's what happened to me and other Black women that I know.

The *Video Vixen* or *Jezebel Black Woman* is the hypersexualized Black woman. Her name comes from the Bible, where Jezebel was a queen who turned her husband against God. Since the dark days of British colonialism, the Black woman has been sexualized and always in the most derogatory of ways. And in relation to mental health, this has caused many Black women to feel increasingly objectified and often demoralized. And if you are a Black mother who feels demoralized, you may experience feelings of helplessness, or hopelessness, or giving up. Also, society may view Black women, and even Black girls, as more mature and less innocent than our white peers. It is frightening to know that even my little daughters may be viewed in this light. Less innocent may lead to being less likely to be listened to or believed.

When it comes to racial equality, there is yet another minefield for Black women. In our professional life, we might find ourselves being the 'first Black woman' to have achieved a role that we have worked hard for, very often overworked for. Growing up, my Nigerian mum never failed to tell me, 'Sandra, as long as you have this skin, you will always have to work ten times harder than your white counterparts' – something that never quite sat well with me, then and now. This can set up an enormous amount of anxiety as we feel that we must constantly prove ourselves to be twice as good as a white man or woman in any role. Imagine telling your young daughter that even though she is conditioned to run this never-ending track of trying to be the best, she will only ever receive crumbs for the utmost effort, not to mention feeling like all eyes are on her, waiting for a slip up, just to be called angry all over again. And very often, it does push me back into the Strong Black Woman role, to defend my ability, and to survive.

Very often a Black woman will suffer in silence and tell no one and add exponentially to the anxiety that she feels by not reaching out for help or for justice.

What does Black Motherhood mean to me?

Normally, you would think there is just Motherhood, almost like this shouldn't even be a question because Motherhood should just be Motherhood, and the funny thing is before becoming a mother myself I would have most definitely agreed. However, this is a thing. Black Motherhood is a thing.

I remember when I was pregnant with my second child, I had opted to give birth to her in a birthing centre instead of the usual delivery ward. There had to be an induction for all mothers giving birth in the centre weeks before we were due to deliver. I had to go by myself as my husband couldn't make it, but I remember getting there and at first I didn't even realize I was the only Black person there. All I saw were parents all taking a look around and admiring the beautiful birthing centre and imagining the day they would be there bringing their seeds into the world, just like I was. Then the time came for us to sit down and be spoken to. I had taken a look around the room as we had to sit in a circle and literally just smiled at the rest of the expecting parents, once again not really focused on the fact that I was the only Black person there because actually all I saw were parents, just like me. Out of nowhere a question was asked, and that question was 'How many people are here today on their own?' My hand in response went up because in fact I was there on my own, and in that moment it hit me: I was the only Black person there. Why did it hit me? Because my raised hand had no company. I was the only person that put their hand up because I was the only person there on my own. Prior to that, I had been so chatty with other parents that it had not at all occurred to me that I was the only one indeed there on my own. Suddenly, I was filled with embarrassment because although I know I'm married, the families there were both parents present and all I could think was they must be thinking, 'Typical Black single mum doing it on her own.' For that reason, for the rest of my time there on that induction day, I felt the need to make my wedding ring highly visible and I made sure I brought up my husband in conversation enough for them to know I was married but not too much for them to know I was embarrassed.

To some, it may seem like this is nothing but a projection, insecurity or a 'me problem', but then you have to think: why would this be a projection? Where did this insecurity come from? Why is this how I had to feel whether it's a 'me problem' or not? Being a Black female comes with certain stigmas and this is one of them – the expectation to be a single mum. I felt the need to defend my position. The funny thing about this is, I already have a child but nobody there knew me; they knew nothing about me except the most obvious thing: I am Black, and to them I am a Black mum and alone. This kind of defence was not foreign to me; the assumption that I was a lone parent was one I had experienced one too many times with my firstborn, so perhaps this was truly the source of my projection, but the latter part of this incident is what being a Black mum is to me – defending.

Before I continue, I just want to say that there is absolutely nothing wrong with being a single mum and I completely take my hat off to those that are doing it alone because it takes a different level of strength. So my issue wasn't that I had a problem with being a single mum; it was more that I don't want you to assume that I am a part of a statistic that you created for me.

– *Tobi Oyedele*

Racism as trauma

Feeling inundated with all of these stereotypes means that, as a Black woman, I am faced with daily struggles of how people perceive me versus my reality. Should I just surrender to what society has deemed me to already be? Should I simply accept being labelled as angry and strong, or reduced to just a sexual being? Or can I really share that I feel wronged, distressed, aggrieved without being disregarded?

The feeling of being instantly categorized with a preconceived stereotype has definitely triggered my depression, and very often hasn't given me the strength to speak out.

As I write this book, it's obvious by looking around that racism is all over the news since the case of George Floyd and then the movement in the UK to remove statues of people connected with the slave trade. As a result, it seems as though the trauma of racism has heightened for us also, both indirectly and directly.

I can tell you about the hundreds of little and not so little things that happen to me as a Black mother every day, just by virtue of the fact that I am not white. Being pushed in front of in the queue, being ignored in conversations, being overtly abused with racist language. We have already mentioned George Floyd and clearly that is as bad as it can get. As I am writing this, the trial of his murderer has just concluded, with the white police officer being convicted on all counts. Even if we're not directly being abused, watching abuse happen to other Black people is as painful, as devastating, as suffering the pain of the attack directly. Imagine my daughters Zoe and Chloe, casually out grocery shopping with me, and them witnessing their mother being subjected to racial microaggressions or openly racial comments. Like the time when a random white lady said she liked my faux locs, then proceeded to touch my hair. By that point I had had enough, because it was the second time that had happened that week. I told her never to touch 'our' hair again. She then said, 'Who do you think you are?' The whole shop was staring at our altercation, including my daughters. I told her that what she did was racist, which she denied, and she then ended up calling me racist slurs – ironic.

It's tragic because as wrong as it is to racially abuse someone, it is equally wrong for a child to see their beloved parent treated in this way. And this is where the anxiety starts.

Because of some of these public conversations about racism and microaggressions, I believe that from the time of my first pregnancy to now that I have a five-year-old, the stigma associated with seeking help for anxiety among Black women has slowly become less difficult. Women have now started to appreciate that a Black woman who is anxious is just that – not crazy or off her head; she is simply anxious and with good reason.

Being a protector as a Black mum

Black Motherhood to me also means being a protector, again of yourself and, more importantly, of your children. It is no secret that being born Black, we already have a fight on our hands, and whereas we try to negate this fact in order to reduce any form of negativity, unfortunately it's a fact we have to face. Before your child is born, you are already worried about what your child is going to face in life, and although that is a mum thing as a whole, regardless of what race you are, as a Black mum that worry is doubled, tripled even. It's one thing to be a protector as a mum, as you most definitely should be. It's another thing entirely to be a protector as a Black mum.

– Tobi Oyedele

Being stereotyped as a Black mum

Becoming pregnant has been one of the most eye-opening experiences I am still going through. I found myself being stereotyped at the beginning because I am single, Black and pregnant. I also found a lack of social support not just because of Covid but because it was hard to network and find people in similar situations. As a Black mum, I feel society sees me in a certain way and expects me to act in a certain manner. Society puts a lot of pressure on Black mums to be good, strong parents, but for some reason the fathers are not held accountable, which I find unfair. With all this, I have also felt extremely empowered as a Black woman; I have networked and found great people who really empower me day to day. Moving forward, I will put my main focus on the positives wherever they come from.

– Shirley Bramble Nash

The right help and the right language

As a mother, if I could get the most ideal support, it would need to be from a professional who would understand my issues from a cultural point of view. Imagine that you told your therapist that you were tired of being seen as a Strong Black Woman and they, in their ignorance, suggested that you stop going to the gym! Oh, believe me, it's happened before. Or imagine having to explain to a professional, over and over again, what everyday racism feels like, and how this is an additional stress factor – exhausting for many. We shouldn't be amplifying Black women only when we discuss anti-Black racism and systemic oppression. We should be amplified, believed and not overlooked *regardless*, without feeling like our struggles are a fetish. Constantly having to explain our struggles, culture and lives in exchange for care and concern is draining. It can often feel like we're fighting systemic oppression by ourselves – isolating us even further. I long for the day that Black mothers can talk about how beautiful and magnificent music is, how we enjoy creative arts, how we have a passion for cooking, sports, writing and chemistry, and *still* receive appropriate and gentle care.

The Motherhood Group started delivering cultural competency training for many reasons, but one of them was that Black mothers are persistently confronted with inaccurate images that others often hold of us. Many of us scream for society to see us for who we truly are, not just stereotypes. Instead, see every aspect of us: our carefree side, our angry side, our loving side, our anxious side and our exhausted side.

Being constrained by stereotypes is harmful.

Cultural competency is crucial because many Black mothers' experiences with mental health issues are often connected to our unique cultural and ethnic backgrounds. It seems as though the healthcare system is geared up to recognize and identify postnatal depression in white women, but when it comes to Black women it's as though the colour of our skin obscures what is going on underneath. Healthcare providers often fail to notice, let alone treat, postnatal depression (PND) in Black women. And it is not only PND. There are studies that strongly suggest that clinicians have greater uncertainty when diagnosing emotional problems and depression when they are presented to them by Black people.[30]

Maternity services should use inclusive language that sounds less stigmatizing and scary! Ask the right questions, and ask a Black mother how she wants to be supported – practically, rather than this blanket tick-box notion of support. And in return, both she and her family will feel more comfortable to ask the right questions too.

I have had my own experience and, in my darkest and most desperate days of depression, I know that I was not identified as being depressed even though the fact that I was should have been as visible as a flashing warning light on my head. If I was white, would things have been different? I think they would.

As a Black woman, I know now that I'm less likely to be identified as depressed, and that is simply because clinicians use tools to screen for PND that were mostly developed following research on participants who were white women. Nothing of this research was applied to diagnosing me or to any other Black mother suffering from PND that I have come across.

As a Nigerian-British young woman, the culture I was raised in looks at mental illness in a very different way from how it is viewed in the West, especially in recent times where there has been a big push in bringing issues around mental health out of the shadows.

Growing up, I can honestly say that I never heard my mother or any family member speak about depression, anxiety or any other mental health challenges. Now, facing my own struggle and being a new mother, I was reluctant to use the term 'depression' and instead I would say 'I didn't feel like myself'. In hindsight, I also had and did complain of physical symptoms, such as headaches and stomach aches, which I now know are also symptoms of depression and anxiety.

Some might say that language and conversation related to depression or other psychological difficulties in African and Caribbean households trivializes these issues, or leaves them unacknowledged – causing many Black children, teenagers and adults to suffer in silence. I often felt that Black families I knew, especially the older generation, didn't open up enough to have those necessary conversations with their kids about mental health. I know I needed those conversations as a child, but they didn't happen. It was as if the concept of mental health did not exist, there's nothing wrong, lives could be crumbling all around them, generation after generation – yet we would still hear 'God is in control', and 'everything is fine'.

Black little girls grow up to be Black women. Some of us have become mothers, and the transmission of information among Black mothers about psychological challenges may or may not have taken place even within adulthood.

That being said, it would be insensitive of me to not acknowledge that there is also expertise about mental health within the Black community, with Black professionals and advocates who work tirelessly to improve communication about mental health. However, only 9.6% of qualified clinical psychologists in England and Wales are from 'ethnically diverse' backgrounds, in contrast to 14% of the population.[31] Of that 9.6%, how many are Black? Having more qualified Black mental health practitioners is imperative for addressing how information is spread in Black households about mental health, as well as the inequalities that Black mothers face.

The view that many Black people have formulated about healthcare and the healthcare system is still based on fear. Also, the notion that Black people don't experience postnatal health challenges has just started to be dismantled. As ignorant as it sounds, and as educated as I was, I still believed that only white women experienced PND, and that PND was considered a sign of weakness that did not represent a legitimate illness. I could easily say I was sad, I was tired, I was demotivated, I was not feeling myself, or I was feeling a bit down – but I could not and would not admit that I had PND. The term 'postnatal depression' felt and sounded too clinical for me to wholly digest. It left a harsh taste in my mouth when I whispered it to myself. I didn't feel it was a socially accepted phrase, and using it only pushed me to worry about the triple stigma I believed I would be in receipt of if I admitted it; rejection from my family, rejection from society and my own internalized self-stigma. I just wasn't ready for that and thought it would make my situation even worse.

I just prayed that someone could see that I was struggling, could click their fingers and say, 'Okay, my dear, you are suffering from... and we can sort that out!'

The truth is that none of my signs were identified by any health visitor, despite them having prolonged contact with me. My symptoms were overlooked and I endured them in silence. I said nothing and neither did they. I'm sure someone might say, 'Well, you should have spoken up', but when you've been conditioned to internalize everything, second-guess yourself, in fear of being the angry or sometimes crazy Black woman, you learn to keep quiet. But surely they should be in a good position to recognize a new mother struggling with PND, put a name to it and help me get treatment for it?

I have, as you can imagine, done a lot of research into this and some findings have suggested that some Black Caribbean women do face difficulties describing or talking about pre- or postnatal depression due to their tendency to under-report their psychological feelings. Just like me, barriers to health-seeking behaviour relate very much to the reluctance of some Black women to admit their problems even exist. This and the way in which, when they do, those problems are dealt with contribute to the problem.

When I did go to services, it did seem like a one-size-fits-all approach. Professionals were not asking the right questions, it's like they have a script, they are not trying to figure out what is good for the mother, it was a disingenuous blanket approach... I was overly disappointed and dissatisfied, considering I was a new mother.

> My overall feeling is that Black women are simply not offered the
> same opportunities to engage with services.

> – *Angela Ajiboye*

I know that cultural understanding of PND is also a big factor, and
by that I mean how West African communities conceptualize PND,
describe it and make sense of it. For a health visitor, midwife or
GP, a depressed Black woman might present to them with signs of
depression but might not describe their symptoms in the same way
as the Western parameters habitually used to assess them.

Time pressure

Thinking about my own dark days in the grip of PND, there were
several things that happened – or didn't happen. The first thing I
noticed was that there was never enough time for me to gather my
thoughts and arrange them and then speak about my pain. When a
person is depressed, they are going to take longer to get through to
and longer to draw into any kind of meaningful conversation about
what is worrying them and what symptoms they have.

Doctors and patients both agree that there isn't enough time
spent at appointments. I often felt as though I was shuffling from
one doctor, midwife, nurse to the next, and the focus was always
on my baby, not my own wellbeing – like a mother on a conveyor
belt. Where any issue around mental health is concerned, there is
the recognition that it will take longer to get to the bottom of it
and get the patient to the point that they are ready and able to talk
about what is at the root of their problem.

I read with a sense of déjà vu the statement of one mother suffering from postnatal depression who said:

> I did go to my GP once and broke down uncontrollably but he

said I have run out of time; you are obviously depressed and must come back which of course I never did and they never contacted me. It has never been mentioned since.[32]

There is no doubt that the way women are treated varies a lot across the board, depending on many factors, and that applies even within the same GP practice. The fact that the woman above was not followed up after she had broken down in front of the doctor seems appalling – after all, the next time the doctor saw that patient it could have been a much more serious situation.

Educating healthcare providers on the experience of Black women

Healthcare providers need to educate themselves on the experiences of Black women before conditions improve for our mental health; it is not a Black woman's responsibility to educate white people on racism and our culture. So, before anyone demands answers, they should listen, observe and read first. Remember, we are walking away from fulfilling the demands of the world. Without careful attention, many Black women will go un- or underdiagnosed, forced to bear a superwoman persona.

How is that fair or just?

During the process of writing this book, I watched a television news story about the rates of Black women's miscarriage, which are significantly higher than for white women. I thought about the midwife who served me through both my pregnancies, and who reported my husband and me to social services. Would she have cared enough to catch early warning signs? To report to doctors if I had been in danger of miscarriage?

I look at my beautiful daughters, and I wonder what would have happened if something had been different. Both my pregnancies were difficult, both births traumatic. I was in so much pain.

I had third-degree tears on both occasions. What would have been different if I had been a white woman?

A study in *The Lancet* analysed the data of around 4.6 million pregnancies in seven countries and went on to suggest that being Black increases miscarriage risk by 43%.[33] I was not surprised. It's not that being Black increases the likelihood of miscarriage, but it increases the risk of not having quality care and attention.

Because there are no official figures, miscarriage estimates could actually be much higher, but it was found that women who had had a miscarriage were more susceptible to encountering health risks in the future such as thrombosis (blood clots) and heart disease; they were also more likely to develop depression. That led me to look for the factors that were known to increase the risk of miscarriage.

I learnt that women are more likely to suffer a miscarriage if we are under 20 or over 40, have had a previous miscarriage, are very overweight or underweight, work night shifts or very long hours, smoke, drink a lot of alcohol, and *if we are Black.*

When I set out to write this book, I intended to speak directly from my own experiences. While I assumed other Black mothers encountered similar prejudice and difficulty, I was unprepared for the levels of neglect that many Black women received from health services and the medical community at large.

Where the NHS is concerned, time is always at a premium, it seems, and that applies right across the board. But there really does seem to me to be no hope of ever improving the situation for the Black woman suffering from PND without more time. Time needs to be allocated to the initial and continued consultation with a midwife, health visitor or GP. If white women are identified as having PND and given the appropriate help, is that because they get more time? Are they easier to identify? Do they speak up more and trigger the right responses from healthcare professionals?

The next failing, as I see it, is the approach of the tick-box exercise. I am sure that a lot of time and money is spent formulating these helpful check lists, but for many women they simply don't work. The health professional goes away feeling content that they have a tick in every box, while the new mother like me is left screaming internally for something, anything, to alleviate her pain and misery.

Another tendency that I have observed is that once a baby has arrived, all the attention will be on the child and their milestones. What weight are they gaining? How much feed are they taking? How are they sleeping? Again, as a new mother, I would be hanging on every word said about my baby, especially about her health and progress, and at the time that was paramount to me. Now, though, on reflection, I can see that often no time at all was allocated to me, the mother, and how I was feeling. No attempt was made to look for any warning signs that I might be dealing with PND. As long as my baby was thriving and doing well, it was job done! My own experience has made me formulate the following ideas that would help to identify any potential problems in new Black mothers, and possibly in other mothers as well.

Suggestion 1. Implement self-reporting statements that could ask the questions that would prompt the new and depressed mother to give answers that highlighted concerns around PND. Of course, I know – and would probably have been guilty of it myself – that honestly admitting to suffering from PND is quite another thing, but surely it would be possible to find a way to ask questions to mitigate the tendency of a new mother to be less than honest about how she is feeling?

Suggestion 2. Be very comprehensive in describing all and any symptoms that might be part of PND, as often I think women like me are totally unaware of the symptoms that might be encountered, such as the stomach upsets that I mentioned earlier.

Suggestion 3. Raise awareness of cultural identity and the part that can play in a woman's experience around childbirth and more training given to health professionals in recognizing cultural norms when it comes to expressing distress and relating individual experience. I say this because even within a single ethnic group there is likely to be variability in the expression of symptoms from woman to woman. It is also true that Black women tend to present and talk about the somatic symptoms of PND more – pain or shortness of breath, fatigue or weakness, insomnia or restlessness.

Of course, these somatic or physical symptoms could be related to any number of illnesses, and it is certainly true to say that clinical recognition of depression, whether PND or any other type of depression, will be higher when a patient presents with psychological symptoms and distress rather than just the physical symptoms.

Black women and high-functioning depression

I, like many other Black women, believe that society encourages us to prioritize other people's needs before our own. This comes with a heavy cost – our own suffering, internal brokenness and our survival mode permanently being kept on.

Black women and high-functioning depression seem to be an ongoing theme whenever I listen to the stories from my community of Black mothers. And as uncomfortable as this correlation may seem, it's a contributing factor to why depression doesn't get diagnosed quicker or at all for Black mothers like myself. Very often, we minimize our issues until we bubble up with anxiety, oversteam with depression and explode – then we find ourselves being dragged into crisis care for our mental health issues when we can no longer hide them.

Smiling, excelling, overachieving, striving for perfection, performing our utmost best, yet toning ourselves down, conscious of not being 'too much' as we don't want to upset someone with our striking presence, all while experiencing the paralyzing internal symptoms of depression – this is something I've experienced my entire life, not only on my motherhood journey.

Even within employment, Black women feel we always have to put our best foot forward, without a fleeting moment to rest – fearing that if we reveal our authentic selves we'll be fired in a heartbeat. And the worst part about this work-related anxiety is that statistically we are more likely to lose our jobs, which makes this fear even more of a daunting reality.

I always felt that as a Black woman, I didn't get the privilege to make silly mistakes or dress down at work despite formalwear not being a requirement. I always put myself forward eagerly for additional projects, went on CPD courses, I came in the office early and always left last – just to prove I was working extra hard, harder than my white counterparts.

Despite this, I didn't feel I was met with the same empathy as my non-Black colleagues. Instead, I was met with hyper-criticism. I was seen as aggressive, intimidating, a threat – something which I internalized and carry to this day. My white colleagues would be able to wear casual outfits and be met with compliments on how quirky they looked in formal meetings. I envied how relaxed and unbothered they felt, being able to just be themselves without the need to over-analyze. When they were late, although they were certainly never praised for their poor time management, I noticed they received something that Black women hardly get – grace.

That still bothers me, we just don't get the same grace. You never feel 'good enough' and are constantly on edge. You lose who you truly are daily – to impress people who you feel aren't committed to seeing or understanding you fully.

But as Black women, we learn to wear our high-functioning mask, we don't have a choice – we have to make sure that anyone and everyone but us is comfortable.

This scrutinization and internalized suffering tears you apart, slowly and painfully, over time, adding to our mental health issues. And it saddens me that there isn't much research on just Black British women's mental health. Many studies compile all ethnic minorities as opposed to solely focusing on the complex issues that Black women face.

If there was more research, we could be better equipped to help Black women recognize mental health symptoms in ourselves. Symptoms which might sometimes look like massive productivity, sacrifice, compartmentalization, hyper-focus, feeling like we're failing and neglecting our own needs.

Many times, we feel our depression is misinterpreted as anger, attitude and defiance. Even if we're crying, trembling or silent.

Not only do we need to receive more grace from society, we also need to give ourselves more grace. We need the support, the space and the time to breathe, remove our masks and find our resting place to reflect.

Black mums, they aren't hard to reach

Black mums,
They aren't hard to reach,
The only problem
Is that society needs to re-teach themselves.
Reach deep deep within themselves
To ask the questions
To learn the lessons
That will lead you to help a Black mother in need,
And please,
Please

Don't come with mere performative allyship
If I can be honest,
With you,
For a second...

We're sick of it.

Completely sick
And when we tell you we're sick,
Listen to it!

Because we're losing our lives
It's been too long
That we're more than
Four
Times more likely to die
When for the first times in our lives
We're truly needed to be alive.
We're truly seen with eyes of love,
That look up to us
And trust.

Black mums
They aren't hard to reach
They come to you,
In your surgeries,
Your hospitals.
Your social care offices

You so sure you care, officers?
My son hasn't done anything wrong,
No, please.
I'm his mum,
Don't shoot my baby, in front of his mum.
No please put down that gu...

I digress,
Well, not really,
I just skipped a beat,
Because even when their babies grow up

The stress doesn't leave.

Will my son survive the streets another day?
Will my daughter give birth and live to see another day?

Black mums,
They aren't hard to reach,
They come to you in their sleep,
They're screaming and shouting,
But you cannot hear them speak,

They may say to you, about their dreams,
It's a straitjacket I'm in
And I'm on a tightrope
If I fall now, I've got no hope
To save myself
And well, is it even worth it
All I am to you is another BAME,
Tut, I mean another name, in a folder upon a shelf.
Yet still here I am
I'm pleading with you for a little bit of help.

And so you help – with the best that you have
But it's not enough
You've educated yourself
You studied hard.
But it's all just fluff
The statistic are clear
Year after year,
Awareness without action

That's why you speak out,
Speak loud,
Speak often.

The 'I can't relate', 'I'm uncomfortable',
It hurts, to feel this way,
A fatal burden,
A mental pain,
It's Black Maternal Mental Health Week,
I'm asking you, will you rise up with us and speak?

– Chaneen Saliee

What do you have to be depressed about?

What do you have to be depressed about?
You have everything.
A roof over your head,
Food, water, a husband, children and most importantly – God.
Sandra, what do you have to be depressed about?

Dear Black families, depression, anxiety, mental health issues
    exist, and are very real.
As real as it gets.
And no, it's not a 'white man's disease',
Mental health does not discriminate.
When we raise our issues, please don't:
Brush it under the carpet,
Shun it or the person speaking up,
Dismiss it and call them 'ungrateful',
Laugh and make light of it,
Or say it's attention seeking.

What do you have to be depressed about?
Sometimes, there's no reason.
And that's the point.
Depression does not care about the beautiful life you've created,
Or the life that others would die for,

Sometimes, it's just there.

– Sandra Igwe

For many of our parents, their circumstances of coming to England from Nigeria, or any other African and Caribbean country, to build a better life for themselves and children, were extremely difficult – starting life from scratch, living on a council estate, experiencing the far more overt racial tensions in the 80s in a country that made them feel critically unwelcomed. I even heard stories of people shouting out to my parents, 'Go back to Nigeria!' This happened while they studied at night school, worked any job they could get, at ungodly hours, to pay for their higher education, and for necessities, as they balanced family life. For them, their mental health was not a priority. There was no time to be depressed when they had to hold on to life by a thread. Listening to my mother's stories often made me think, it's true, *what do I have to be depressed about?*

But, as I said:

Depression *does not* care about the beautiful life you've created,

Sometimes, it's just there.

So we should all listen, and understand what each other is going through.

My experience is that a young Black woman suffering from depression will go to almost any length to avoid her mother and older relatives finding out. Of course, while many families would go out of their way to find out more about what was ailing their young women, so that they could help them, some would not.

If I were talking to a friend who was dealing with depression

What I have learnt is that no parent is perfect (whatever that may be). None. No one mother and their children are the same as the next. Which has led to me understanding that just because one mother seems to have it all together, it doesn't mean that you too should have it all together.

Life and circumstances change constantly, and you may be at that point and part in your life where you need more support than usual.

And there is absolutely nothing wrong with that.

In fact, it is a great opportunity to reflect on how things are going and make changes if and where necessary. Sometimes you do not realize how bad a situation is until you have come out of it at the other end and have looked back at things from a better position. Only then can you be grateful for having gone through the hard times and process.

If I were talking to a friend who was dealing with depression, I would say take yourself back to when you were pregnant with your child and going through labour. Months went by with certain sacrifices, changes to the body and discomforts along the way.

As you are getting bigger, even more changes occur and adjustments need to be made (such as new clothes, shoes, abstaining from certain foods, alcohol restrictions, swollen feet and the rest).

And then the day comes when you are in labour. Contractions became stronger and more intense as the time came closer to having your child. Skip forward to some minutes, hours or days, at the point where your child was finally placed in your arms, and all that pain was worth it. All the changes, sacrifices, discomforts and more were worth it, knowing that you did what you could to keep yourself strong enough to have your baby and to hold them in your arms.

The only difference this time is you need to do it for your mental health.

You have to go and grow through some changes, discomforts, removing toxic habits, people, and making sacrifices in order to give birth to the healthier version of yourself. It's okay not to be okay, but it's not okay to continue living in an unhealthy state because it seems easier to continue as you are. You can do it!

Taking that first step in helping yourself and helping your child/children is usually the hardest but one that you know would greatly benefit both your child's/children's and your wellbeing.

I have found that the suggestions below have helped me greatly, alongside compassion for yourself for when you fall back into negative ruminations:

- counselling
- going for a walk, especially in a park with loads of trees and nature
- having a mini clear-out, one room at a time
- listening to some of your favourite songs
- prayer
- talking to a trusted family member or friend
- meditation
- reading
- listening to a podcast
- joining a social group, such as The Motherhood Group
- social media detox
- exercise
- daily journalling
- art therapy
- taking a long bath with essential oils (lavender, rosemary or eucalyptus), Epsom salts and baking soda
- deep breathing techniques
- cognitive therapy
- going to a comedy show.

What I have found is that because these options can be done on a daily, weekly, monthly and yearly basis and most are free or low cost, it makes it easier to incorporate them into your life.

See what works best for you and stick at it. If you do not feel as though you are seeing much improvement, then try something else or get advice from someone who already does and see how they overcame the hurdles you may be facing.

With most things, if some form of foundation has not been established and set in place, then whatever is built on top will soon fall apart. Or at least will be harder to build upon – that is for sure! And that is exactly how your mental health should be looked at. By also having a support system that understands the ups and downs of your particular motherhood journey, you have already equipped yourself with one of the strongest tools you can on this journey of being a parent.

I for one found this concept initially hard, as I was very used to being independent and not having to rely on anyone when it came to doing simple things like going to work or socializing with friends. Then, suddenly, you find yourself having to plan and organize things that were once very spontaneous and did not need a second thought. Being a single parent forces you to have to give things more than just a second thought, and that in itself can be hard to adjust to and difficult at times. I call this organized momentary freedom as that is what you need to do sometimes. Organize some time to be 'free' of the constant stresses that come with motherhood and fill your cup back up, so that you are not left pouring from an empty cup.

– *Yvonne Ihegborow*

Another study on this subject written by June Brown and colleagues was published by the *International Journal of Clinical Psychiatry* and was titled 'How Black African and white British women perceive depression and help-seeking'.[34]

This study had found that detecting psychological problems in Black African people had been observed to be much lower than it was with white British people and even with Black people of Caribbean origin. It also found that little research had been done on the factors that make the Black African sufferer from mental health more reluctant to seek help.

The authors found that Black women often thought that being depressed even for a long time would not be likely to lead to any serious consequences. Black women also associated being depressed with fewer symptoms and thought of it as something that would soon pass. They were also much more reluctant to ask for any help or treatment. Over half the Black women who took part in the study said they would not look for any help with their symptoms of depression. Most of them said that a big reason that contributed to them not seeking help was the difficulty they had in consultations with their GP or other health worker.

Lots of the women looked for other ways to deal with their depression rather than the medical route, and it was not working.

Somehow, we need to put an end to the stigma and encourage a better understanding of what mental health issues are, especially PND.

And although we were less likely to use maternal mental health services, complete treatment, improve or achieve full recovery, I believe that should not be the end of the conversation but the start. That's why I was so eager to start an awareness week in the UK – Black Maternal Mental Health Week – not just to highlight the disparities that we face as Black mothers but to also ensure that Black women get the mental health and maternity care we deserve during and after childbirth, and that the gaps between maternal mental health services and the community of Black mothers and birthing people are bridged, to share and develop resources for increased access to mental health services for Black mothers and to raise awareness of the barriers that Black mothers face in accessing support, which can contribute to postpartum depression and anxiety.

Services should exercise flexibility around appointments, offer more time and more choice, make use of community groups and resources already out there. For the woman who does conjure up the confidence and strength to ask for support, who is the most at risk, services should believe her, not ignore her or keep her on a never-ending waiting list where she's more likely to disengage. Services should work with groups who already understand Black women, because they *are* Black women. No one will need to worry if there is knowledge of the language spoken, values held and beliefs shared of our community.

I remember with my second daughter, I had a better understanding of my mental health and wellbeing. I spoke to my GP about support options available for a mother who was having mild difficulties with stress. He seemed so unequipped and really unbothered. This is no surprise when I read that GPs are less likely to refer Black mothers for psychological therapies because of difficulties in communication, cultural differences in the way that mental health symptoms are presented, different explanatory models for distress being held by GPs and cultural stereotypes that lead to misdiagnosis.[35] In fact, that was the first and last time I mentioned anything as such to my GP. Health professionals should recognize and value diversity in another, then appropriately adapt the support, giving her the tailored care she deserves. They shouldn't be afraid to ask where in Africa or the Caribbean islands we're from, what faith we practise, if we practise any at all, our background, family structure, culture, as we may feel like they're getting to know us better.

After my organization launched the awareness week, and I became a Trustee of Birthrights and the Co-chair of their National Inquiry into Racial Injustice in Maternity Care, I was asked by so many organizations, charities and government bodies, 'How can we support more Black mothers?' Then I would take a quick look at their staff, and they're the most undiversified set of staff members you can come across. Some often prided themselves in being 'diverse', but the one Chinese or Indian colleague did not represent me – not in the slightest. I mean, the only similarity we had was that we were not white. Once these services really and truly have a diverse team that genuinely want to understand about the local communities they serve, who are curious and respectful of cultures, who understand that a Black mother does not operate under a one-size-fits-all approach, but comes in a variety of forms, with her own experiences and preferences, then outcomes will improve for Black mothers.

Black mothers will not feel marginalized from accessing quality and effective mental healthcare.

Black mothers will feel less alienated and hopefully will feel empowered to trust services again.

When I think about how Zoe and Chloe might be treated by the NHS someday, I feel a hole open up in my heart. How could anyone look at my girls and not want to protect them, keep them safe and well? I've seen too much to expect perfection from doctors and nurses, but they need to step up when it comes to Black maternal care and mental wellness.

My job is to love my girls and prepare them for the world, which includes (if they choose this path) becoming mothers someday. 'It's okay to have big feelings,' I tell them when they cry over ice cream or scraped knees. 'It's okay to need support.' And it is! Perhaps telling them to trust and feel their emotions now will set them up to expect better care as mums. They won't try to do it all alone.

Then again, I want Zoe and Chloe to have realistic expectations of becoming mothers. It's hard! Your physical body changes, and often, your mental health suffers. Having a partner helps. Having a community helps a whole lot.

Having children confuses things, and a lot of women lose themselves for a couple of years. I did! It's easy to fall into depression and grieve over your old life. When will I feel like myself again? When will I come up for air? Why is this so hard?

If I give them the information up front, I hope Zoe and Chloe will have a better understanding of how to overcome maternal struggles. Every Black woman's experience will be different, but we all deserve attention.

Services have to prepare for the next generation of Black mums to receive higher-quality care, especially when it comes to mental wellness.

Being a Black mum to me is having to constantly defend

Part of what being a Black mum to me is, is having to constantly defend – not even your children but yourself as a mum. The story I shared is something that happened before my baby was born. If it's a fight at that stage, then how much easier do you think the fight becomes? In the early stages of motherhood both times, I found that if I wasn't defending myself with people from my own community then I was defending myself from health officials because of the decisions I made due to what I knew as an African. Let's talk about this community thing real quick! I find that no matter how old you are, African adults that came before you tend to think you have no idea what you are doing and must criticize everything you do as a mother.

At first I tended to take the criticism, no matter how much it annoyed me, but I drew the line when an adult who had seen me at church breastfeeding my then four-month-old baby told me that I had to burp him and how I should do this. I had been doing this mothering thing for four months; if I didn't know how to do anything else, I would have hoped and prayed that burping a child was the one thing I knew how to do – otherwise, what had I been doing for four months? So at this point I said to myself: Tobi, speak up. I literally had to check this woman because one thing you aunties can't continue to do is come for me and what I do with my child; I had to defend myself as a mother – otherwise, it would have continued. It is a scary enough job bringing a little human into the world, but when every single thing you do is questioned, laughed at or criticized, then eventually you will crumble because you will go on thinking you do not know what you are doing. Nobody should make you feel useless as a mother, especially when you know you are doing your best. I had to stand up for myself that day and every day after that for this reason. I am the one raising my child, and although it is wise to seek advice when needed, it is highly unhealthy to have to constantly be discredited for everything you do as a mum. Defending yourself as a mum is not necessarily a bad thing; I would most definitely say that it is most times a very necessary thing, because there are times when you have to put your foot down and let people know you know exactly what you are doing, and if you don't, you have access to those who can help you.

– *Tobi Oyedele*

CHAPTER 4
Shame and Weakness

The Strong Black Woman Myth

Nine months of waiting,
Waiting and longing to meet the one,
The one who will change my life.
Good things come to those who wait.
When you arrived, I cried.
I cried tears of joy and tears of 'how'
How would I raise you?
To be the girl that I wasn't.
How would I be the mother that you deserve?

Strong.

But with you, I learnt about my strength,
With you I learnt perseverance,
And with you, I learnt courage.

– Jenny Temenu

Black women aren't born strong. We come out of the womb as soft and vulnerable as anyone else. Over time, we build walls to protect ourselves from the expectations of white men and women, Black men and even often other Black women. The world demands us to be perfect mothers, smart career women and strong caregivers for our partners, children, parents and community, but I can't possibly be all those things at once. I'm not superwoman. In fact, often, I'd like to be saved.

In Igbo communities, mothers, grandmothers, aunties and cousins beam with delight when you get pregnant, give birth and mother your children. Because children are deemed the ultimate blessing, other women can assume you're doing a brilliant job taking care of your blessing gracefully – 'Look at you, Sandra, just a perfect mum!' – but I struggled daily with expectations versus reality. I'd been taught my whole life that Black women were strong, stronger certainly than our white counterparts in every aspect. What did it mean if I couldn't take care of myself, my babies and my husband without feeling as though I was falling apart?

I believe that many people in my community grew up believing that mental illness is not a big issue, save for *overt* displays of mania or schizophrenia. People pulling their hair out in the street. Women screaming like demons. Even then, some genuinely believe mental illness is more of a spiritual issue. As with physical health, which often is managed in the home with spicy nutritious foods, herbs and rest, we are sometimes encouraged to solve our own mental or emotional problems, without the aid of doctors or mental health specialists. 'Why are you crying?' aunties ask. 'Your life is so easy compared to what I had growing up. Be grateful for the blessings that you have.' Which sometimes can feel like a translation of 'Shhh, endure gracefully' or 'Don't embarrass us' – essentially, 'Be a Strong Black Woman.'

When I struggled with dark thoughts and anxiety after giving birth, it felt as though it was brushed off by those around me. Many had never been familiar with the concept of postnatal depression (PND), let alone assuming I could fall under it. Wasn't that the sort of issue that only affected white women or weak women?

I'm sad to say this was my thinking, too.

If I had known about PND *before* I got pregnant, I would have viewed it as a sign of weakness, maybe even selfishness. How dare a woman focus on her own needs rather than those of her child? Now that I've suffered from PND, I can't believe that was my perception. Women aren't self-indulgent for caring about their own emotional and physical needs. We're just human. When I first started to struggle with my emotions after Zoe was born, I was too ashamed to tell my friends. I stopped returning phone calls, stopped watching television and hardly went outside. My husband was working long hours, providing financially for his new family while I stayed home. Why couldn't I be grateful? Here I was, a woman with her own successful career, on maternity leave, in a new marriage, with a roof over my head and a beautiful daughter. I had everything going for me. What valid reason could I have for being depressed, let alone postnatally depressed?

I remembered what my mum had told us as kids whenever we refused to eat our vegetables that had been put in front of us. 'Finish your food; poor children would love to eat what you're eating...' Why couldn't I just be grateful? *Get it together, Sandra,* I told myself.

I thought I could *choose* to be happy in the same way I'd chosen to eat vegetables as a child. Of course, depression isn't something anyone would choose. I was trapped by the expectations of Black womanhood that had been placed on me by my community, society and the world at large.

As I have said before, suffering from mental illness is not something that Black communities in the past have readily acknowledged or prioritized, and there is certainly a heavy stigma attached to it. That is especially true when it comes to PND.

Did my emotional pain make me a raving lunatic? Would it make my family ashamed of me?

It makes you dangerous as a mother

I am a Black woman, and for most of my life I have understood mental illness as an unfortunate affliction. I've a deficiency that enfeebles the overall character. It diminishes your personal value, as a child, a sibling, a wife. It makes you dangerous as a mother.

I have fought depression for as long as I can remember, my first spell occurring during adolescence. I could not understand the feelings of emptiness, and I hid the ugliness and pain. After a while I began to recognize it as a yawning hole inside me; it came out at night as shaking sobs, salted tears, stifled in the darkness, under the covers, in my bed, in the room I shared with my sister. In my teenage years and young adulthood, it came out as self-harm: ragged cuts on my wrists and thighs.

But Black girls don't do that.

Later on, as a young woman, it made its mark in substance abuse, self-hatred and self-sabotage. Some time in my 20s, I sought help from my family GP. A mild-mannered Yoruba man and a colleague of my aunt, he looked me up and down. 'But you don't look depressed, my dear,' he said gently. I did not even truly know what depression was, but I knew that I was not being seen clearly. Despite that, it would be many years before I made another trip to the GP for depression.

Part of the problem is that suffering is not understood when it inhabits the body of Black women. It's almost as though there is no language for it.

What is understood is that we should not name our pain. We are to suffer in silence and should not demand that others acknowledge it. When we communicate our pain outwardly and become mentally ill, it breaks with the stereotyped understanding of what a Black woman is: a beast of burden, tirelessly toiling without complaint, that survives.

But we do not survive endless cycles of hardship and abuse, whether it be experienced at home or as casualties of this system. We do break, and we break down.

Still, the Black woman is not afforded fragility and sensitivity, not even in the imaginations of her own kinfolk. Her mental illness becomes an issue of weakness, shame and failure: a weakness of character and spirit, a shame to her family and a failure of personal motivation to overcome difficulty.

Attitudes are starting to change now, but where they lag behind, there remains tremendous, unnecessary suffering. Black women are still being failed within their communities and without, and the real shame is that we are being let down, time and time again. The real failure is that we fall short of supporting Black women in their journey of recovery. Families need to provide a safe space for Black women wherein they understand first and foremost that mental illness does not detract from their perceived strength. If anything, it adds to it.

Race and unconscious bias, depression, motherhood – what did that look like?

I wouldn't say that I suffered from full-blown post-partum depression, but having experienced depressive episodes many times in the past, my doctors felt I was on the brink of a relapse after the birth of my children.

I would say that I just narrowly skated past it. I was down, up and down, for a long time, and I very much struggled to keep my head above water with young twins during a pandemic.

Depression can make you feel like taking to bed for days on end. Of course, with young babies you can't really do that (thank goodness) but some days maybe the most I could manage would be feeding the babies, loving and nursing them. Maybe I couldn't get them dressed, or shower myself, or tidy the house.

I felt I was carrying the burden of unconscious bias on my shoulders. I'm a Black mother, and I didn't want people to think I'm a bad Black mother. Many of us just want to be received with the same open-mindedness and open-heartedness that white women are afforded in their day-to-day interactions with the world. Instead, as Black women we're portrayed as one-dimensional tropes of badness, hardness (and therefore strength), laziness, fecklessness and other undesirable and untrue characteristics. These tropes seem obvious and cruel, but they infect the minds of all of us.

I often felt I couldn't afford to take it easy on myself, for fear that I would be judged as a bad mother, particularly because of my Blackness. Because isn't that how we're judged? Aren't we often punished rather than supported when what we might need most is help?

So, I leave no room for doubt. I rarely leave the house with my children without making sure their skin is smoothed and shiny with coconut oil, their clothes fresh and clean, and their hair turned up in silky, coiled puffs. I want onlookers to imagine the time that goes into the preparation of each child. When they take in the details, I will them to know of the dedication, and from there, to understand the effort, the love, the care.

The opposite of fecklessness. Good mothering.

That's the burden I've shouldered. The struggle is obscured by a glossy outward appearance, and so they cannot know how much it takes out of me, and how difficult it can be on a low day. And even if they could understand, wouldn't they think that I could take it, because of my Blackness?

– *Zara Oteng*

When a baby is born to an Igbo mother, the community jumps in to focus on the thanksgiving of the baby. What a blessing! Pride and favour to the parents. In fact, the more children a couple have, the more they are considered to have been blessed with wealth and fortune. And unfortunately, a couple without children are usually frowned on by the community. However, if the baby fails to thrive in any way, the mother will feel blamed. 'Her baby cries too much. He looks too thin. Feed him more. Wrap him up.'

As a new Black mother, I felt the weight of expectation and surveillance heavy on my shoulders. I was a young Black woman with her life in perceived order, expected to take to motherhood as automatically. But I'd always been a career woman. At the time, I loved to work, travel and also bask in my creativity. In some ways, giving birth made me feel that life had been stripped away and replaced. I was only a good woman insofar as I was a good wife and mother.

What I remember most about the time after birth is guilt. Guilt that I didn't feel the way I thought I should. Guilt in case I didn't manage to breastfeed properly. Guilt if my baby developed even a hint of a nappy rash. Guilt that I didn't jump out of bed each day with a spring in my step.

To make matters worse, I was still recovering from the trauma of the birth itself. My birthing plan had gone out of the window the day that Zoe arrived. I'd gone back and forth to the hospital multiple times begging for doctors to admit me. *Something is wrong*, my brain said. The pain was unbearable. Everything I'd been taught about keeping my emotions in check dissolved in a flurry of panic. 'I'm not leaving!' I finally screamed when the front desk attendant asked me to go home again and return when my labour was further along. Would a white woman have been treated this way?

I hated that I'd been driven to act like the raving lunatics I'd always been warned to avoid. I was supposed to be above this! A powerful Nigerian mother-to-be. A career professional. A Strong Black Woman. Yet the hospital nightmare would not end. I was induced without my consent. Then my epidural failed. 'Please,' I begged the midwife. 'I can still feel it.' Nobody believed me.

You're not acting like a good Black woman in pain, I imagined them thinking.

Black women and girls learn very early that their tears mean little to most people. We're not met with empathy. In fact, we're often treated worse for showing emotion at all. At one of my first jobs, my former manager harassed me openly. She screamed at me on the phone one day, and even sent colleagues directly to my house to berate me on two occasions. 'This is unacceptable,' I told HR while crying frantically. Ultimately, I had to hire a union rep – a white man – to represent me, before my complaints were taken remotely seriously.

After such a traumatic birth experience, the hospital simply sent my husband and me home to recuperate. I felt numb. I had trouble bonding with Zoe. Much later, I researched what steps are usually taken to help women in my position. I learnt that any woman suffering from perinatal issues around depression or mental illness should have access to talking therapies and treatment as a matter of urgency. For some women, leaving these conditions untreated could be dangerous to the woman and her baby.

I won't recommend a one-size-fits-all approach to supporting the Black maternal experience. Black women deserve to be cared for. We deserve to be vulnerable. Healthcare services need to understand that for some Black women, mental health is a very sensitive issue, to be approached with empathy. Many of our families and others are sceptical of professional support being used against us, and many have learnt to associate mental difficulties with weakness.

I dream of never being called resilient again in my life. I'm exhausted by strength. I want support. I want softness. I want ease. I want to be amongst kin. Not patted on the back for how well I take a hit. Or for how many.[36]

Falling through the cracks

Of course, for any woman to receive treatment for a perinatal mental health issue, she has first to be diagnosed. In my case, this was difficult. I never went to a doctor for a formal diagnosis. I'd already learnt that health services felt indifferent to my literal shrieks of pain. They'd even sent a social worker to investigate my home after the midwife accused my husband of abuse. Why would they feel differently about my mental health? Indeed, many Black women find it difficult to trust and confide in healthcare services. We might not present or express our symptoms the exact same way white women do, on whom the studies have been based. As a result, Black women tend to 'suffer in silence' because we fear medical malpractice and abuse.

Another issue is the lack of continuity in health services. GP services assign patients to whichever doctor is in duty, rather than doctors with whom the patient already has a relationship. Black women, and especially vulnerable Black mothers, need to establish safety with a professional before we can open up about our mental health problems.

In one study, GPs were asked whether or not the women they were consulting with had suffered from previous mental illnesses.[37] Over half said they would not be confident to report an answer. (I myself had previous struggles with depression after my beloved aunt died.) Most of the doctors said that they relied on the patient's notes to tell them, although they also admitted that relying on these notes was risky. But if many Black women feel pressure to handle their own problems in silence, how can they get the support they need when reliance is mainly on notes? I know from my own experience that it can take time to unpack the feelings we have. Black women are not emotionless machines, but we need the time and space to be vulnerable, to let our guards down, to be open.

Moreover, many GPs who responded to the study said that they had not had any specific training in perinatal mental health, and of those GPs who had undergone any form of training, only 25% had undergone the training as part of their specialist GP training. Another 33% had studied the issue, but as part of their own personal study.

A small minority of the GPs said that their own 'lived experience' or extra training that they had accessed had helped them be more effective in helping women with perinatal mental health issues. In terms of the day-to-day work of the surgery, just over 25% of GPs felt that perinatal mental health was a high priority; just under 50% said perinatal mental health was 'on the order of business'; another 25% said that when it came to perinatal mental health issues, there were too many other competing issues for them to deal with or they didn't have the ability to make the issue a priority.

For Black women, who already feel ostracized by professional services, it can be so difficult to get the help we need from doctors who sadly don't make our mental health a priority.

When struggling after the birth of my first daughter, I tried to reach out to my GP one day when I had plucked up the courage to speak to someone. I quickly changed my mind. *Sandra, what are you doing?* I thought. *He can't help you.*

Back to the Strong Black Woman (SBW)

Soft life, embody me

This year I've made a promise to myself that the 'soft life' will embody me,
More than ever before.
The phrase 'Strong Black Woman' is not and will never be a compliment,

Despite the fact that I've often felt like I had no choice but to be...
  strong.
Don't praise me for my strength,
Glorify me for my resilience,
And applaud me for the struggle I was preconditioned to
  endure.
Black women, we are not invincible.

I am so much more than my trauma.

And I pray that I will never preach the Strong Black Woman
  rhetoric to my daughters.
They will grow knowing they can be vulnerable,
Soft, sometimes.

So, don't be surprised if you see me,
Taking even more breaks,
Choosing comfort over distress,
Enjoying my nearest and dearest,
Asking for more help, unapologetically,
Giving myself more grace, and permission to be,
Me.
To be seen, and self-compassionate.

– Sandra Igwe

Ever since I can remember, I felt obligated to appear strong, keep my emotions in check, not accept help, find enormous worldly success and care for others over myself. Yet living this way put me in real danger. It made me feel small, broken and lonely. When I see my white social media friends and white counterparts post about their struggles online, I think, *It must be nice to be believed and supported.*

My big dream for myself – and for other Black women, if they want it – is to allow myself to become more delicate and vulnerable. I aspire to be seen as precious both by my Igbo community and by health services. I aspire to be helped. I aspire to be rescued. I aspire to prioritize my health and my happiness. I aspire to be as soft as flower petals.

How much easier would my life – and the lives of my daughters – be if we laid to rest the myth of the Strong Black Woman once and for all?

Virtually no statistics and no studies have been done on how Black women deal with stress and how to evaluate that stress. My own theory is that we Black women suppress our emotions because we learnt early that they don't serve us. When Black schoolgirls cry, teachers ignore or chide us. When Black daughters cry, mothers tell us to be grateful. When Black mothers cry, health professionals threaten to send social services. It's exhausting and often confusing.

Not only are Black women expected to be perfect mothers, but we're often asked to take on more than our fair share of caregiving roles. Older Black women are sometimes the harshest critics of younger Black women when we don't sacrifice ourselves on the altar of caregiving. I hear aunties talk about spoiled girls who don't look after their ageing parents. 'She is so selfish. After all her mother did for her.' I listen to grandmothers complain that young ladies in my generation are not as dutiful as they once were.

I admit that I wasn't the most enthusiastic caregiver. When my daughters wanted to play with toys with me for hours on end, after a few moments, I would think, *How much longer until I can scroll through Instagram? Take a nap? Make dinner?* I had to re-mind myself that doesn't make me a bad mum, but simply an adult woman with other obligations and desires outside motherhood. For a long time, however, I couldn't integrate my desire to be a perfect caregiver with the need to care for myself. In my mind, a lot of

Black women, who live with the expectation to be SBW, suppress our own needs to meet the expectations placed on us.

Where did this all come from? No woman wakes up one day and thinks, *Right, I am going to take it all on, I'm going to be an SBW and undertake all the obligations I can.* Some of this is learnt from older female relatives. I grew up watching my mother taking on the full identity of being a mother. If you asked her what her calling and purpose was, she would simply say being a mother. And I assumed the only path forward was to emulate her. I wanted to be like her and my aunties. I was never aware of my mother being under any stress, but looking back, I wonder if some of her perceived strength was a coping mechanism. No, I take that back, it *was* her coping mechanism. Was she scared to show her true colours to us, her family? Did she ever want to openly cry or scream? Would my life have been different if I'd seen my own mother break down and ask for help in our presence? Would I have been more comfortable asking for help with my mental health after the birth of my own daughters?

For Igbo communities, there is a fear that asking for help makes you vulnerable. Aunties tell their children, 'Don't shame us!' at every turn. Whether in Nigeria or the African diaspora, Igbo people try to put their best foot forward. We wear our best clothes and put a smile on our faces when we go outside. We must be the best. A daily prayer point I remember growing up was that I will always be 'the head, and not the tail, at the top, never at the bottom'.

I grew up knowing how difficult it was for us to ever admit that we needed something from anyone outside our own immediate family or community. A sense of pride and secrecy. The pressure to perform and achieve success and self-sufficiency was and still is immense.

It's not that Black women don't realize we've been typecast. None of us want to take up the mantle of a stereotype. But how should we even begin? Do I refuse my responsibilities to my children? My parents? My community? Do I let people down to keep myself afloat? What about my husband, who has his own pressure to provide financially? Is he supposed to take on my responsibilities, too? Yet as someone who grew up seeing so many strong women around, I wonder what would happen if we all simply said, *Enough is enough.*

One woman that I spoke to remembered in detail all the things that her grandmother did when she was young, and the work that she managed to get done without the aid of any mod cons.

This lady got very animated as she spoke about the memories she had of her grandmother and what she remembered seeing her grandmother do and not do, work all day and complete everything on her own without complaint. I asked her if her grandmother had ever shown emotion or broken down and cried, and she looked shocked, as though the very idea was ridiculous. But as we spoke some more, she began to realize that the model that her mother and grandmother had shown her was the role that she had fallen into. With a tear in her eye, she remembered that her grandmother had shown no emotion even though she was badly affected by painful arthritis and later by severe heart disease. Never once did she see her grandmother cry or give in to any form of self-pity.

As I've said before, Black women, especially those of us who are financially stable and otherwise in good health, are expected to grin and bear it. We're expected to take on burdens that aren't rightfully ours – a sick parent, an ageing community member – in addition to our responsibilities as mothers. We shoulder the burden of resilience. We create an invincible exterior to face the world. No chinks in the armour. We forget to take care of ourselves, and we can't trust those around us, not even health services or sometimes even our own relatives, to help.

What doesn't kill you, makes you stronger,
That's a lie, a lie often told.
To keep us as hard as iron,

Firm, unshakable, masked up.
Until we eventually crack, snap,
Tap-tap out, lose our minds.
Shame, loneliness and stigma – it didn't kill me,

But it burdened me,

Made me lose my identity,
Lose the will to speak.
It didn't kill me, but it shook me.
Shook my nervous system,
Trapped me in my thoughts,
Kept me in survival mode,
Pushed me to the brink of depression,
Anxiety-filled perceived strength is better than dying right?
Let's grin and bear it...
What doesn't kill you, makes you stronger.

– Sandra Igwe

Single Black mother

Never in a million years did I expect to be a single mother, because growing up with deep-rooted societal stigmas I was coerced into believing that Black single mothers held no value; that they were broken, dysfunctional and poverty-stricken living on handouts. After meeting and falling in love with my college sweetheart, when we found out that I was pregnant, we agreed that the next natural step was to get married, so in 2007 at the tender age of 19 we tied the knot in a beautiful ceremony in the presence of God, our family and friends. Being a wife and mother was a dream come true, but every time I looked at my son and husband I couldn't believe that this was for the rest of my life.

But my once-fairytale marriage quickly turned into a living nightmare that I couldn't wake up from. I never knew such feelings of pain existed. My life became the lyrics to an Aaliyah song. The shame and the embarrassment made it impossible for me to articulate what I was feeling and thinking to anyone, so I decided that I would hide behind the mask of the Strong Black Woman to 'make it work'. I felt forced to have to hold back my emotions to avoid appearing weak and pretend that my marriage was a success because the world was watching.

However, every moment that I was alone, I was falling apart. Each morning I would stand at the window with my one-year-old son in tow watching my husband leave for work, paralysed by anxiety and insecurities. Every night whilst having a bath I would lie in the tub and allow the water to wash away my tears. There were moments where the pain in my heart was so unbearable I contemplated submerging myself and never coming back up, but then I remembered I had a son who needed me and would muster the strength to drag myself out of the tub, crawl into bed and cry myself to sleep.

Whenever the health visitors would come and visit my son, I would sit there praying and hoping that they would see me too, but despite my bloodshot eyes, thinning body and silent stares, they never saw me or the fact that I wasn't coping. I was depressed. I would question whether God could hear me because my prayers continuously went unanswered, as the health visitor would come and go like I was invisible. Why couldn't she see me? Was it the colour of my skin? Was it the mask of the Strong Black Woman? Was it not within her job description? I just needed someone to ask me if I was okay. But they never did! Even with them there, I felt so alone and insignificant.

I was now being held together by a single string. That string was my faith. I believed in the sanctity of marriage and wanted to remain true to the vows I made before God and didn't want to raise my son in a single-parent household, so we sought spiritual counsel from our pastors who had been married for decades and confided in them about everything that had been going on in our marriage. Despite the wise counsel we received both inside and outside of church, both spiritual and psychological, my marriage remained intolerably broken. Deep down, I knew that I had to put the health of myself and my son above everything else; I knew I had given the marriage my all, so much so I had nothing left. It was time to go.

In 2010, there I was; the very thing that I had feared had come upon me. I was a single mother, struggling to balance university, settling into a new home, the separation and raising this beautiful two-year-old boy. I had to block out the whispers of church members who treated me like I had leprosy and silence my own inner critic that labelled me a failure. Now this was way before Instagram, and Facebook had only been around for a few years, so the online community of mothers we see today didn't even exist. So, you can only imagine the challenges I faced being a first-time Black single mother raising a son in the UK: I felt isolated, lonely, and attached to my Strong Black Woman mask. At university I didn't fit in as I was the only Black single mother in my group, so when others stayed behind to study, I would envy them because I was always running off to collect my son from nursery in time. When social events were organized, I was never able to attend due to child-care; my family lived on the other side of town and had their own commitments, and I never had a tangible support system. All my finances were tied up in extortionate nursery fees and providing for my son; he was my number-one priority and every decision I made was centred around him. I was his mother, his father, his counsellor, his chauffeur, and everything in between. Every evening I would give my son my full attention and every night while he slept I studied and worried about the future. I knew that I had to work twice as hard to build the type of life I wanted for myself; I knew that as a Black woman there were not a lot of opportunities out there for me. So, when I graduated with a bachelor's degree in psychology and began to navigate a career in health and social care, I found that I had to continuously prove myself and my value. I became very intentional in my every action and even the words that I spoke to avoid falling into the stereotypical pothole of the angry Black woman – bitter, angry and mean. I would be overlooked for promotions because of my gender and race, but I was educated and determined, and that empowered me to work at a level of excellence that made me relentless.

The single thread of faith that had held me together during my traumatic marital experiences remained and began to weave together every broken piece of me. God wanted me to be whole – spirit, soul and body. I relied heavily on the Word and the Holy Spirit for parenting values and guidance on how to raise my son in a godly manner, ensuring every Sunday he was in children's church, that he was seeing strong Black men in their rightful place as priests of their households and spent time with his uncles and grandad, because as much as I loved him as his mother, I knew that I wasn't a man so I couldn't teach him about manhood and masculinity.

My son needed to see positive male role models for his personal growth and development. I enrolled him in extracurricular activities to equip him with the life and leadership skills necessary to promote discipline, confidence and independence. As my son got older, I experienced heightened levels of parenting stress because I grew concerned about his safety and survival, from being racially profiled by the police to the gang culture that plagued inner-city London; both encounters could lead to him losing his life. But I put my trust in the Lord because He promised to be a father to the fatherless and I have never looked back since. My son is now 13 and I believe that everything I have instilled in him and exposed him to has enabled him to have greater feelings of self-worth and better social and academic achievement.

Overall, the challenges I faced being a single Black mother have taught me the power of resilience, that you can bounce back from challenges, adversities, pain, disappointments and the uncertainties and fears of life. You do not have to be defined or imprisoned by the negative stereotypical views of a single Black mother or be burdened with the myth of the Strong Black Woman. But that you can redefine what the single Black mother experience means to you, make it what you want by creating your own narrative, it's yours and belongs to you. Just because your marriage, business or relationship has failed, it doesn't make you a failure, no matter what the world says. Now my Strong Black Woman mask sits on the shelf collecting dust, because I no longer hide behind it but stand in the wholeness of who I am, I am clothed with strength and dignity, and I can laugh at the days to come. I am valuable and worthy of love, joy and happiness. I recognize that there is strength in my vulnerability and transparency and that there is power in sharing my experience with other single Black mothers as it's vital to come together as women to educate and empower one another so that we can overcome and challenge the stigmas and constraints of today's culture and traditions.

– Stacy Gacheru

Overlooked

Sometimes, my husband and I talk about our joint struggles. As a new father, he felt immense pressure to provide financial support for our family. 'Sandra, I *have* to work the long hours.' I feel immense pressure to provide emotional support. There were times when I called myself a single parent because my husband was always working. I wonder about the sympathy I might have received as a mother without a partner, someone who wasn't assumed to be above needing help. Maybe my treatment would have been exactly the same – who knows? But what I do know is that I felt overwhelmed and overlooked, because everyone assumed I was more than fine.

I recently heard a story of a Black woman who had had a caesarean section and I went to hear what she had to say about her experience. I thought about my own birthing experiences, how, during my second birth, the doctors refused to give me pain relief. I pulled my hair out in clumps begging for an epidural. I was simply ignored, written off as a raving Black woman. When Lorraine told me about her own awful surgery, my mind railed. *This could easily have happened to me.*

'I could feel the surgeon cutting,' Lorraine said. 'The surgeon told me that it was just pressure, but I knew it was pain. I felt so helpless.'

Lorraine's experience left a mark, one that I relate to as a woman whose medical staff ignored her during labour. I asked for the bare minimum – to be attended, listened to and given pain relief. None of it came to pass. My second daughter was born so suddenly that nurses urged me to immediately open my legs wider to avoid cutting off her oxygen supply. Imagine how much less traumatic the experience could have been if I'd not been expected to be a Strong Black Woman.

Am I a Strong Black Woman?

The infamous Strong Black Woman character. Am I her? At times. However, societal pressures make you feel as though this should be your default setting 24/7. Regardless of any issue that occurs, personal problems you may face and the countless doubts that cross your mind, you are supposed to know exactly what the answers are and be able to handle it alone. Because that is what a Strong Black Woman would do, right?!

This is where the damage begins. Because, before I was given the chance to find out if I have the capabilities of being a 'Strong Black Woman', I was a Black Woman. And before it was determined in my mother's womb that I would be a girl to grow into a woman, I was Black. And with this comes a plethora of connotations that I had absolutely no choice in adhering to or at the very least having to consider all the time.

All of this seeps into the type of experience you have as a Black mother, especially coming from a family that is very matriarchal. A family of many women who all have their own experiences of motherhood, and at times under some crazy circumstances too. The pressure and struggle was real. To be fair, for the most part that pressure came from myself in not wanting to look like I cannot cope because my circumstances are looked upon as easier than theirs. At least you were born in this country, at least the NHS is there ready to help with any issue you may have, at least you have a room and bed to yourself, at least, at least, at least.

And I want to make it extremely clear, gratitude is definitely felt in those moments when you look back. However, raising a child in the 1970s/1980s in comparison to raising a child in the 2000s definitely comes with some differences and challenges. My reality as a mother and their reality as a mother both exist as opposite and colliding truths. They both come with their struggles, trials and difficult moments. Some of those difficulties we would be able to understand and some we would not be able to relate to, even if we tried.

In addition to this, the idea that being a Strong Black Woman involves not leaning into your vulnerability as a woman has to be one of the biggest lies and myths told to Black women. As time has gone on, I have learnt that there is another level of strength in admitting to yourself and those around you that you have reached your limit, that you are anxious about a particular decision that you need to make on behalf of your child, and so forth.

To be 'Strong' as a Black mother is not to run yourself down and try to take on the world by yourself. To be a Strong Black Woman is to understand that we all have a part to play in this world and that we are in fact stronger together than we are apart.

– Yvonne Ihegborow

Musings of Honest Black Mothers

Motherhood is a journey, it's deeper than a title

Motherhood. I learned how to be a mother like most mothers do, on the job, referencing the glorious matriarchs that had gone before me. Trying my best to live up to their spotless record of excellence. Armed with familiar prayers, holy scriptures and legendary anecdotes of my mother's journey into motherhood; acting as a fading map, providing me with guidance.

My introduction into motherhood was nothing picturesque. It was everything that could probably be described as a perfect disaster. Nothing could prepare me for the hurricane that reality was bound to be. I'd spent years dreaming of the moment I'd see the two lines informing me of my new title – mum. Pregnancy was supposed to be so very special. 'It's a beautiful time, it brings you and your partner closer together,' I was told.

I didn't get much of a chance to experience any of the highs. I spent the majority of my pregnancy bent over a toilet vomiting, or crippled by nausea forcing me to lay on my back at a particular angle.

Hyperemesis gravidarum (HG). At my worst I was vomiting between 10 and 15 times a day. Unable to eat, drink and sometimes even urinate without a sudden impulse to vomit. I felt my body was betraying me. None of the strong mothers I had seen had ever experienced anything like this. I became so depressed. I was strangled by the isolation I felt as no one understood what I was going through.

'You're not sick, you're pregnant' I heard more times than necessary. I spent hours crying, contemplating whether to take medication in the fear I was harming my baby. I remember things coming to a dramatic halt when I suddenly collapsed in the supermarket, suffering from dehydration and low blood sugar levels. I was convinced I'd died in that moment. As the sound slowly became muffled and my sight grew more and more blurry, I felt as if I had already failed as a mother. *How was I going to keep my baby safe once out of the womb if I couldn't even guarantee my child a meal on a daily basis?* I often thought to myself.

I'd uttered every prayer my fragile heart could construct; I grew extremely frustrated with the reality of my situation. Nothing was changing. Things just intensified as the baby grew, all the milestones I'd patiently awaited zoomed past without an opportunity to acknowledge or enjoy them. I was unable to have the beautiful photoshoots and the bump update Instagram posts, or the loving first Mother's Day where you're made to feel so special.

Motherhood is a journey. It's deeper than just being a title. It's an opportunity to live again, not through your child but with your child. It's a chance to have conversations to soothe your inner child. I have since learned that my personal journey of Motherhood is very much about confronting my own childhood. It's about creating the experiences I yearned for, the tropes I'd see in movies but could never experience because Mum was working night shifts or couldn't afford to do it exactly how I'd seen it on TV.

It's been two and a half years now and I have a daughter who is the sunshine of my life. Her smile inspires purpose in me and propels me to go above and beyond to ensure she lives a life she can feel proud of. I was able to see my pregnancy through because I have an incredible mother, who did her best to try to understand me when healthcare professionals were dismissive and when my employers downplayed my experience with HG.

I was fortunate to be reminded of the fact that I have everything I need by way of a community of mothers who I can lean on. That community of mothers is made up of aunties, friends, godmothers, grandmothers and so many others who see the value in being a part of that village, helping me raise my child.

It is important for me to give my daughter the tools required to navigate her own motherhood experience with ease. One of those tools is language. As a child who is not fluent in my mother tongue, my daughter's time with her grandmother goes beyond being spoilt with cupcakes and sweets. It's a time in which she is fully immersed in our Nigerian culture. She is taught what the taste of traditional Akwa Ibom cuisine is made up of; how the inflections and tonal sounds of the Ibibio language should really sound. As much as I try to give her my very watered-down take on all things heritage, I do my bit by giving her the rituals and rites of passage as a young Black girl growing up in London. In that field, I am more than an expert. She is being taught the necessary skills to survive life in South London. I do my best to prepare her for the wondrously wicked world that exists beyond the safety of our home. At two years old she already shows a curiosity about the nature of why things are the way they are. She is aware of her skin; she has been showered with compliments and history about the richness of her radiant brown skin. I teach her to see herself in her absolute fullness and to embrace everything about her – internally and externally.

One day she will ask me why things are the way they are. My only hope is that by then, I won't be explaining the fact that I don't know.

I hope to be able to explain the multitude of reasons why, despite the way things have been, knowing who you are will cause you to only ask the questions that truly matter.

– *Kahlia Bakosi*

A Black woman with a black son who has additional needs

Feeling isolated as if no one else understands what we go though,
Especially being a Black woman with a Black son,
A son who has additional needs.
Most of the services I access in regard to his additional needs,
Have little to no diversity.

This journey has been life changing,
And has given me a real sense of accomplishment!
But it comes with its challenges.
Having to fight for everything on his behalf,
And not taking no for an answer.

Having to work ten times harder than parents who do not have
    a child with additional needs.
I feel as if Black parents who have children with additional needs
    are a forgotten community and really have to advocate for
    their children in a way that others may never know.

But when I see my son do things that the doctors said he
    wouldn't,
When I access things for my son that they said I couldn't,
All while I teach my son how to be proud of himself and who he is,
I feel empowered.

I take pride in breaking down barriers and paving the way for
    my son, and other children and parents who have additional
    needs to make the journey easier for them.
I want to do the hard work so they don't have to, and they can
    just be free to be who they are.

– Tiffany Jade

Memoirs of an honest mum

Sometimes
The fear of failing just seems to
Overwhelm me
The what ifs and the I should ofs
And maybe I'll try it this way thoughts
Run marathons in my head
But the truth is Mummy doesn't have all the answers
And I'm still figuring this shit out myself

Don't let the dark days
Stop you from shining
Remember
The sun also has to set
To rise again
You are much more than your sadness

You ask me how I am
And I so badly want to tell you
How anxiety is bruising me
It keeps pulling me and shoving me
Into corners made to trap me
I want you to see how hard I try
To hold back the tears

How hard I can feel my eyes straining
With lack of hope
From not being able to hold off that cry

But your simple how are you *is distasteful to me*
It just rolls off your tongue
Without meaning

Without love
So, I am forced to mutter
I am fine

When your limbs feel weak
And your voice sounds discouraged
Don't you forget
Your presence alone
Is strength for somebody else

You see
There isn't a name or expression
To describe the intensity of my pain
My confusion
I just know that I once felt whole
Whatever whole felt like
And now I feel emptiness

– Hilary Speaks

Who told me I have to be perfect?

Being a mother is one of the most difficult jobs I have ever had. I love my kids, I do, but that doesn't always make motherhood any easier. I won't pretend to have 'cracked the code' to motherhood – I won't even pretend to believe that there is some one-size-fits-all blueprint to navigate how to raise human lives. Motherhood is something I am still learning. As my kids grow, there will always be new lessons in motherhood to learn.

As a mother, I often feel like I'm being asked to be all things at all times. I have to set boundaries – both for the development of my children and for my own sanity. I have to be a mum whether I am happy, sad or tired. I have to be a mum even during the times I have no desire to be me. I have to be a mum, which is to say primary carer, even at the times when I am desperate for someone else to take care of me. I have to be a mum when I am at my lowest, and sometimes that means I have to be fun (for my children) whether I feel like it or not. I won't lie: it is not easy.

I often find I cannot escape the anxiety of wanting to get things right from my children's point of view whilst worrying that I am somehow letting them down. The kids seem fine to me, so why can I never shake the anxiety of having to do right by them?

Do I maintain a cordial relationship with my kids' dad, having heard and witnessed the internal struggles of friends, family and strangers who grew up without a father figure? Do I cut my kids' dad off completely, knowing how complex that relationship is for me? I swing between these two extremes on a daily basis.

The thing about motherhood is that I am constantly having to make decisions that are in the kids' best interest, my best interest, or (luckily, sometimes) both. The easier decisions are the ones that benefit my whole family. Those are much simpler and less anxiety-inducing to make – though they still come with their own challenges.

The thing about motherhood is that I often have to make choices that go against my best interest. My sister introduced me to some philosophy by Simone de Beauvoir, a text called *The Second Sex*. Without getting into it too much, Simone says that women are the only ones who have to put themselves on the backburner to nurture someone else's life.

I heard that loud and clear.

And this is why decision-making as a single mum is so hard. There is nothing I want to do more over the weekend than have a lie in. It feels like I barely make it to the end of each working week. I'd love to spend all of Saturday in bed. But I have young children who need to go out, be active, touch grass, generally do things and see the world outside of our home. So even when I am exhausted and would rather shut out the outdoors, I get my family ready: comfortable shoes, warm clothing, snacks – and we set off outside.

I want to show up for my kids.

I want to show up for myself.

Often, it feels like I can't do both at the same time.

I am in my dream job and I am happy about that.

But am I putting my career before my kids?

Am I still allowed to have selfish goals?

Do I, as a single mum, still have the choice to dream for myself?

Yes, my career helps me to look after my kids. But trying to balance a demanding career with caring for two young toddlers and all their wishes, interests and demands is a lot. Sometimes I am so exhausted by motherhood that I'm not sure how to cope.

Yet, when the kids stay at their grandparents', I sit in my home and cry.

Motherhood is a never-ending rollercoaster.

As a mum I spend my days travelling between the really high highs and the debilitatingly low lows. Some of my worst days are when I have to be at work early but have had no sleep. Or when the kids are throwing a tantrum over a toy and I can't remember who's turn it is to play with it. Or when I raise my voice at the kids, and immediately feel a pang of guilt, because I know there's something else bothering me. Motherhood is hard.

Motherhood is also one of the greatest blessings I have ever received.

There are experiences I've had with my children that remind me of the true meaning of love. Like when my kids and I go to a safari park and have a lovely time. Or finding a new forest for all of us to explore. Or picnics in the park on a warm summer's day. There is so much to give thanks for.

I chose to be a mum and I don't regret it. I want to enjoy motherhood, and I want my kids to enjoy having me as their mum.

I am constantly putting myself down for my failure to be 'perfect'.

I am constantly judging myself for falling short of my aims.

Who told me I have to be perfect?

Are we not all human?

Are we not all flawed?

I know the idea of a 'perfect' mum is idealistic and unrealistic. I am learning to make peace with that. Motherhood takes so many twists and turns but, at the end of the day, I choose to find beauty in the chaos.

– Tash Li

Motherhood has always been perceived as this blissful experience, but yet they fail to mention the cries us women go through, the postnatal depression, the anxiety, the hard days, the days you have the panda eyes, the way your body changes, the stretch marks, the days you feel unappreciated. However, these are all clothed with a smile. Today I stand with @themotherhoodgroup on Maternal Mental Health.

When I found out we were having twin girls I got so excited. I immediately started thinking about all the perfect little twin pics I would take, my friends kept sending me the cutest pictures of girl twins on Instagram and I imagined my baby girls taking those perfect twin pictures.

Then the girls came, I did so many mini shoots with them and my girls refused to let me have that perfect twin pic I'm like girls this isn't what I imagined the twin life photos to be

I listened to a podcast earlier this week and the guy said a lot of the times we're unhappy or disappointed with certain things in our lives because it wasn't what we pictured our lives to be like. But the thing is sometimes the problem isn't the circumstances in our lives, it's the picture that we have in our head of what it's 'supposed to be like'. So what we really need to ask ourselves is where are we getting the picture from? Sad truth is, a lot of the time we get the picture of what it's 'supposed to be like' from Instagram, and when things in our life don't look exactly how we see it online we think it's not right.

If you feel things aren't going perfect like the way you imagined it to be in your life, like the perfectly curated images you see on Instagram, it's okay, it's not all supposed to be perfect all the time.

– Gloria Sade

Today I post this picture to support all the mothers who have suffered in silence and to stand with the mothers at @themother-hoodgroup because we need to stand up and stand together to make it okay to say 'I'm not ok'. I became a mum at 22 and as a first-time mum I was soooo scared. I wanted to prove to everyone that told me it wasn't a right time for me to have a baby that I could be an amazing mum. I remember rocking Kamron with my foot under the desk in Greenwich University library, saying I needed to get my degree, I remember driving in the Blackwall Tunnel with Kam screaming in the back and tears rolling down my face, I remember feeling sooo lonely because I put my all into being a mother...so the invites stop coming and friends stop calling... I remember being sooo sad and tired I didn't leave the house... I remember so I'll do anything to help new mums say...I'm not okay... and still to this day, some days I'm not okay. #postnataldepression.

– Kandaze Joseph

Birthrights Inquiry call experiences

I feel my race means I am seen as less

I am pregnant and just starting to experience maternity care for the first time. When I'm asked about my ethnicity (African and Caribbean), I am told there is no box to tick that reflects this, so can I pick one or the other?

At one appointment, I was kept waiting for several hours to see a consultant, only to be told everyone had gone home, despite me asking three times when I would be seen. When I challenge this, I am spoken to at the same time by three white staff who say it is my fault for keeping hold of my notes and that I am aggressive. I am scared to deliver in this hospital.

So far I feel unsafe during my care due to poor communication. When potential concerns were found at my scan, I was told to get dressed, as the appointment was over. I had to actively ask what the implications were, and when I did further research, I found further implications that I wasn't told about.

I feel there is no empathy and my severe nausea was waved away with the attitude of 'that's pregnancy, get on with it' and no follow-up or medication was offered, despite me experiencing dehydration following water aversion and vomiting.

I feel my race means I am seen as less, other, expected to endure more. It led to me being called aggressive by someone who has never before met me – three white staff against one lone Black vulnerable female.

– Anonymous

A girl 'like me' should be stronger than that

I've had no issue with my pregnancy care in any pregnancy to date but I believe my race and ethnicity played a role in my first birth and second postnatal care.

With the birth of my first child, I felt my voice was ignored. My expressions of pain and exhaustion were diminished with comments about how I didn't look like I was in that much pain and how a girl 'like me' should be stronger than that. I was told people 'like you' don't need epidurals. I laboured for three days, I was unable to keep food down or sleep at all for 48 hours. I was begging for an epidural and shaking with the effort of trying not to push. When I got my first midwife back after several shift changes, she was appalled I had been left to continue struggling and had a consultant informed and epidural scheduled within an hour of taking over my care. The consultant was also furious no one had mentioned me and what was happening at all before then. I finally had my epidural and I eventually delivered with no complications. The use of the terminology 'like you' felt racial.

For my second child, I had good birth care; he was premature. After we went home, he developed jaundice. My health visitor was not convinced, but my whole family could see it. She said she'd test his levels just to put my mind at ease. He tested super high and the HV was alarmed but she kept insisting the machine must be broken. She agreed to inform her superior, though, still insisting there was nothing wrong but 'mum wants some reassurance'; superior agreed to refer to hospital. At the hospital the doctor admitted the reading was very high but insisted from the look of him there was nothing to suggest he was severely jaundiced, just a 'slight' yellowing of his eyes. By then he looked neon to me. They did another reading and sent his bloods off; it was even higher than the last. My baby was immediately hospitalized for several weeks. The white staff did not recognize jaundice in a Black baby.

– *Tricia Boahene*

I felt safe, but not listened to or properly cared for

I have scoliosis and therefore not a straightforward pregnancy. I kept being seen by different midwives and had to explain my situation every time I met a midwife.

During birth, my waters broke around 3pm. I was sent home and returned around 1am in pain. I was sent to a room to wait without being checked. Around 5am the midwife came to check on me because I was screaming with pain and said I was in active labour and needed to be rushed to the delivery room. It was too late for any pain relief or for the water birth I requested. I was in active labour for almost five hours with only air and gas. My baby's heart stopped beating at one point. The obstetrician was called in and was quite rude and rough. My baby had her cord around her neck and arm holding on to the cord so her elbow was in the way and she couldn't get out. I was cut and the suction cap used to help her out. I then struggled with the afterbirth. The obstetrician almost gave me an epidural at this point, but was thankfully told by the midwife that I couldn't have one. I was almost taken for a C-section to have the afterbirth removed, but thankfully managed to push it out. I was then stitched up and only given paracetamol for the pain. After, I got infection around my stitches at two points during my recovery, but was not given any pain relief. I was given antibiotics twice.

I felt safe, but not listened to or properly cared for. I felt any concerns raised were dismissed and so I stopped raising concerns.

I believe the racial trope that Black women feel pain less led to me being ignored when I was in pain during labour till it was too late for pain relief. I believe this also led to medical professionals thinking it was okay to prescribe only paracetamol to a woman who has had her genitals sliced and two infections after that.

– Anonymous

The midwife did not adequately discuss options with me

My care during labour and at hospital was good and I feel I received good care there. My care during pregnancy, however, was not. I was passed between midwives who very rarely contacted me, if ever. I became very ill twice and both times my midwife either didn't answer the phone or did not return my call, even after being contacted by the triage line many times. While I was in hospital the first time (at around 10–12 weeks) with a kidney infection (the first of many in my pregnancy), I was not admitted to the maternity ward, and no information was given to me as to how my baby was doing/would be affected.

In the final weeks of pregnancy, the midwife did not adequately discuss options with me, and had I not been so adamant with my own research, I would have been misinformed about some things, such as birthing while on SSRIs [selective serotonin reuptake inhibitors]. She did not contact me in the last weeks and 11 days after my due date I called her to check in, and she responded by leaving me an answerphone message saying she'd booked me an induction. I then called her back to say that I did not want this (repeatedly) and she proceeded to use manipulative language to convince me to have it, rather than discuss other options.

During my pregnancy I eventually developed a fear of any healthcare provider, especially midwives. I felt invisible and that they did not care what I felt and what would happen to me. I felt safe in my labour in hospital, after hiring a doula in the final weeks of pregnancy, and having written a birth plan for every eventuality and going through it with every healthcare provider I dealt with while there.

I feel my race impacted on my care in a way that was not obvious straightaway. After speaking to my doula, I learnt about the statistics for poor maternal care for Black women and it clicked that, out of four other women who had children within the same year (four of my friends), I'm the only one who had care like this.

– Laura

CHAPTER 5

'Pray it Away'

Faith vs Mental Health

Christianity is vital to shaping how many Black people live in the UK. Many of us depend on our churches for community, support, direction and meaning, as well as hearing the Word of God, fellowship and a place of true worship. In fact, a church census in 2005 found that Black Christians are three times more likely to attend church than white Christians, and in London 'white Christians declined by 18% over 2001–11, whereas black Christian growth was 32% over the same period'.[38]

As a Christian, I've often seen my faith in Jesus as a central part to my identity. He has been a light in the darkest moments of my life and has filled me with hope when I didn't know how I would cope with motherhood.

I grew up in a Pentecostal church, filled with Nigerians, some Ghanaians and a few Caribbeans, and in many ways, church was a place of safety and comfort for my family and me.

As a child, it was a day I looked forward to, seeing those I genuinely felt cared about me and had a love for God. It was a second home where I sang in the worship team and played with my friends after services. I remember eating plates of delicious jollof rice and chicken they served after service while my mother and her sisters chatted with their friends. As I've got older, although I still believe in casting our anxiety to the One who cares for me, I don't agree with how some churches preach about dealing with mental health and emotional wellness. I feel like there has been a history of a disconnect between mental health and the church as an institution.

If you have severe anxiety? Simply 'pray it away'! And everything will automatically be fine. Many times, the conversation will stop there, but personally, I don't think it should. I believe we as Christians are overdue a fresh conversation about how our faith impacts us and can help Black maternal mental health. But the notion of mental health can still be a highly stigmatizing topic within the church, with many believing that depression is purely a spiritual issue, a demonic attack, with the solution solely centring on praying for healing. Some see therapy and medication as a sign of weak faith.

Mental health – in God's hands

'Sandra, why are you crying? Praise Jesus, the scripture says, "He will turn your mourning into dancing."'

As conflicted as this sounds, my personal relationship with God means that my beliefs centre around God being the creator of life, as well as the supreme authority on matters related to health and wellness. I also believe that I can simultaneously love Jesus as I seek support from doctors, counsellors and therapists. It would be unfair for me not to acknowledge that I have noticed a recent shift in the church making efforts to encourage people to get professional support for their mental health challenges. I've also seen work to disabuse people of the notion that mental health is separate from general health or healthcare.

Be anxious for nothing,
I recite these words, over and over again.

I call on You, as tears drip down from my face,
Laying there with my baby, praying frantically for Grace.
You promise me,
You will go before me,
And you will be with me;
You promise me,
You will never leave me or forsake me.

Why do I feel so broken?

Yet, I hold on to Your words.
You said you have plans,
Plans for my peace,
Plans to give me a future and hope.

Depressed, anxious,
But I look up at the heavens,
And I remember Your supreme presence.
Depression, anxiety –
May never be cured in this lifetime,
But when my time is up, they'll be sadness no more,
Until that time, promise to stay near me,

As I lean on You.

– Sandra Igwe

Emotional release

It would seem easy to argue that many of our parents from African and Caribbean communities didn't have much awareness of our mental health growing up, but they did understand the importance of emotional release – they just couched it in spirituality. When I was little, my mother and family often praised how intuitive I was. I had powerful emotions, vivid dreams and what some might even call clear visions. Intense emotion, if funnelled through the Holy Spirit, is seen as a beautiful gift.

I was seen as often 'too' emotional, with so many big feelings and undiagnosed ADHD (attention deficit hyperactivity disorder). The only safe or appropriate place I felt comfortable to cry or scream was in church. For me and many other people in the faith, crying out to Jesus in times of distress often brought a sense of direction and sometimes instant deliverance.

Later, when I was 12, my mother and I realized that I could sing. I mean *really* sing. My voice was beautiful and strong, and church members encouraged me to use my gifts to praise God. 'Come sing for us, Sandra,' my mum would say, calling me into the sitting room to greet guests. I watched in shock, and a little fear, as my voice provoked real tears from adults. I often wonder if this was the only time any of them could cry without fear of retribution or shame. I didn't realize it then, but my gift – at least insofar as the community was concerned – wasn't just my voice or a time of Spirit-filled worship, but possibly my ability to solicit emotional catharsis.

Over time, however, my troublesome emotions got in the way of my spiritual duty. 'You're not focusing,' I would hear. 'You need to pay more attention to your gifts.' I seemed destined to become a leader within our church community, but I just couldn't concentrate. Looking back, in hindsight, my undiagnosed ADHD drove me from one hyperfocus to another, and I feel like my church family eventually gave up. Sometimes I wonder how others would have interpreted my PND if I'd managed to prove myself as a spiritual leader in the church. Would it have shown how even the most spiritually gifted women need help?

The most religious

From my own experience, I know that Black Christians tend to hold on to our faith, despite our circumstances, and statistics back me up. I also believe that many of us only feel comfortable expressing emotional needs before God and the church. I remember growing up and pastors literally casting demons out of distressed church members with perceived emotional imbalances, some with addictions, others with diseases. I learnt how to speak in tongues and pray a type of spiritual warfare prayer to have victory over my circumstances.

Today, still a Christian, I do often wonder about many of those who stepped forward for deliverance and prayer. What if they had unregulated emotional problems and undiagnosed mental health issues? What if they needed prayer *and* additional support – practical support? I know many who in the past would go to church rather than a doctor, and it hurts to think that they could have received help and medicine if they'd had more confidence in health services.

Another wall that many young Black Christians in the UK come up against is insistence from older relatives that we *have it good*. It's almost as if they simply can't fathom why anyone who grew up in the UK would have any real issues; they must be so small compared with what the older generation went through...

This has always struck me as misguided at best. If someone told you that they had diabetes, a heart problem or cancer, you wouldn't tell them just to pray about it or give it to God. You would surely say, 'Go to a doctor.' We can afford to treat each other with a little more empathy.

Of course, I wholeheartedly endorse that we pray that we or someone we love will make a good recovery from a mental health condition, but we must also be proactive. It simply is not possible to 'pray away' a mental health issue. We need help with that, and

I am proof that strong faith doesn't equal perfect mental health. Religion and faith have a huge and beautiful part to play in our lives, every day and in every circumstance, but there are times when we must also turn to professional services to help us as well. Surely that's applying wisdom – something that the Bible talks about.

Mental illness – a wider issue

Postnatal prayers

And so I fall to my knees
And I pray to a god I'm not sure
I believe in
And I say
Lord, am I broken?
I don't think I feel as I should!
Lord, why can't I find
The Joy in Motherhood?

– Lucy Zion

The church isn't perfect, but it certainly isn't uniquely responsible for mental health issues in the Black community. We need to do better, but we must discuss how Black people, and especially Black women, process their emotional health outside of church. For many of us, the fact remains that Black people aren't always safe outside our church communities.

Mental health issues account for the most morbidities among women during the perinatal period. Obviously, the figures and cases will be reported differently in different places, but the bottom line is that around 10% of women having children have some sort of perinatal mental health issue during their pregnancy. A further 13% of women develop postpartum mental illness like PND, as

I did.[39] No one can argue that Black women don't need to have a solid foundation of mental health knowledge in order to care for themselves and their children.

All the numbers, as I have come to expect, are horrifying. The stats suggested that 23% of women who had died postpartum were suffering from mental health disorders.[40] Worse was to come, as I read on and discovered that suicide was the second leading cause of maternal death in the UK. The consequences of these mental health issues do not affect only mothers. They can lead to low birthweight or to preterm birth and less favourable interactions between mothers and babies. This in turn can lead to children going on to develop emotional, behavioural and cognitive issues. The ripples in the pond of maternal mental ill health can spread far and end up having the most devastating impact on families and the children living in them – not to mention the cost and the resources needed to help women, which will be considerable, to the health services providing them.

I looked more into how Black women who suffer from depression and other mental health issues used religion. Was it always helpful, as the church insists? At an event hosted by The Motherhood Group, one Black mother commented that she had no knowledge of PND prior to birth, and that the expectation to turn to prayer felt unhelpful:

I've had three babies now. I don't know what postnatal depression is supposed to be, how you're supposed to feel, what you should look like, or whatever, I have no idea. What exactly is postnatal depression? What are you supposed to be doing, saying, or whatever? How do I know? What should I do? Pray? Give up?!

Another mother, who was based in the UK and did not have family living near her, said:

I think my PND was a lot to do with the stress and the lack of family or community nearby. I think that Black people certainly will get depression, but I think it is more to do with the fact that I don't think we're allowed to have depression. I think that the Black society is quite a matriarchal society and therefore you've got to cope. You are the one who must sort your family out, and so, therefore, you are not allowed and it is not practical for you to be depressed.

Yet another Black woman shared:

I didn't open up to my family. I wouldn't want to and I didn't feel that I could and I know it's just the stigma. It's just that thing of 'look at that girl'. I just could not have that stigma attached to me. I tried religion and spoke to my pastor, but I can't say that really helped and again I did not open up as I did not even want the pastor knowing that I might be 'touched in the head'. I think stigma in all aspects of a Black woman's life has a lot to do with her failure to flag up when she is in trouble with her mental health.

Spirituality

There didn't use to be many studies on how illness impacts Black women in the UK in particular, although I understand much of that is changing. The depression commonly experienced by Black women can present in different ways and to different degrees, and can be characterized by feelings of unexplained tiredness, misery, sadness or exhaustion. It can lead to the sufferer feeling incapable of even the smallest tasks, losing their appetite, and losing interest in socializing or in sex. It can make the sufferer worried constantly and, especially in the case of PND, feeling a failure and feeling guilty, worthless and hopeless.

They will struggle to sleep despite feeling so exhausted and might even suffer from aches and pains such as stomach cramps and back ache.

In general, in the UK, 4–10% of people will experience depression at some time during their lives.[41] There has been a lot of work done to research the relationship between mental health and spirituality, and that work has mostly been done around depression. In one study, six people had been followed who had been suffering from depression for at least two years with the aim of seeing what role spirituality played in helping them deal with their mental health.[42]

One of the central themes that emerged from this research was whether or not the respondents felt that they had a purpose in life. Isn't having a purpose supposed to keep people from succumbing to depression? Personally, I believe my faith has given me a purpose and hope.

After I gave birth to my first daughter, Zoe, I was a little confused about my new purpose. Although I had this beautiful new daughter to love and clean and care for, that didn't help me get over my feelings of misery and guilt. I had always heard that the solution was to put my faith in Jesus. *Please God*, I prayed. *Just help me get to the next day.* It was comforting to be in communication with God – I've always prayed – but why did I still feel discouraged? Was God really going to help me change Zoe's nappy?

For the purposes of the study I was reading, spiritual care was defined as enabling people to cope. The concept was that having spiritual support meant not questioning what had happened, but understanding what was going on, good or bad, and fitting it in a meaningful framework. One woman in the study commented on the limits of faith in her experience:

When I'm in a phase that I'm able to believe that there is a God who gives meaning to that universe, then I have hope. But there have been spells when I haven't been able to believe that, and that has been absolutely terrifying. That's been falling into the abyss.[43]

I could relate to that and to the fact that this person went on to say that losing their faith led them to ask questions. What is the point in being alive? Why am I even here?

For me, suffering from depression shook my whole foundation. In those darkest days, I could only describe it as looking out on an apocalyptic landscape where everything had been destroyed. Where there had once been the green shoots of hope, there was nothing but grey destruction. It was the strangest feeling because I would be looking at things around me that I had looked at a million times before, but everything looked completely different, all the colour and the joy stripped from them.

But my faith did remind me of my purpose, comfort and meaning when I was in a confusing time. While faith and prayer is a different form of therapeutic approach from professional mental health services, I do believe faith can form a foundation to help restore sanity. I encourage health services providers, even those without strong faith, to work with – not against – the religious institutions and faith-based communities of Black mothers. I heard of a mother saying that when she was in the depths of despair, she believed that she had lost her faith altogether. And although her midwife was not a Christian, the mother talked a lot about her faith and Christianity, and she felt better because the midwife listened. She felt better because the midwife encouraged her to keep holding on to her faith, when she felt like giving up.

I believe that my relationship with God helped me to carry on through the difficult times.

When I was a girl growing up in South London, I knew of a woman who lost her husband. She said her faith sustained her through heartbreak, and she was confident that she would see her husband again in heaven.

While not perfect, faith in God can also help us process grief.

Lack of understanding

Black people of faith don't always have the best experiences with the NHS. The Motherhood Group has conducted questionnaires and focus groups, commissioned by NHS England and Improvement, called 'Engaging mothers from Black, Mixed, Asian and White Other backgrounds' about accessing perinatal mental health services. Some people who have responded to the questionnaires say that their spiritual or religious life is completely ignored by any doctor that they see, and that there is no holistic view taken in that respect, as it would perhaps be of their social life. Instead of trying to convince Black mothers to confide in health services, why not bring healthcare services to Black women by integrating into Black churches?

If we already enjoy the support of faith-based groups, it makes sense to interact with spaces that we already go to. As an adult, I take my daughters to a church that welcomes people of many different cultures and ethnicities. I could've picked a Nigerian church like the one I grew up in. Certainly, there are many wonderful Nigerian churches in London, but I wanted to find a church that fits my current ideas about faith, and share that with my daughters. It's been a joy to take them to services and watch them grow in faith and friendship with others around them. The same goes for the schools they both attend – faith-based schools. Watching them blend education in an environment that understands their faith feels safe and secure to me.

Indeed, congregations are particularly good at offering support to each other. Emotions are a big part of many traditions. Christianity promotes love and forgiveness, hope and contentment, and that can play a big part in helping someone suffering from mental health issues or other traumas. In fact, there is scientific evidence that the neural pathways connecting the endocrine and the immune systems can be affected by the patient feeling more positive emotions.[44] The actual buildings of worship themselves can also play their role in helping somebody who is suffering from a condition like PND because they are associated with comfort and happiness. The same is true for art and music, especially where they are part of faith-led events.

Studies have been done into the power of prayer to help people who are suffering illness. Personally, I think this is a very tricky area to study. If someone is in pain and they are given painkillers, it is easy to study the result of that and the method by which the pain is resolved. If someone is prayed for and they improve, then it could be that the prayer was what helped them, but it could also be that they improved for a number of other reasons. One thing is clear, however, and that is that people who have spiritual beliefs will normally be at lower risk of developing depression.[45] People who have a strong spiritual or religious belief tend to deal better with bad news and with serious health problems. Regardless of which religion a person follows, the most important thing is that the person feels connected and supported by something bigger than themselves during their most difficult times.

For me, it is comforting to know that someone bigger than me, all-knowing, all-loving, is watching me and wants the best for me.

Even people who have no religious belief will often ask for prayers to be said for them before they go in for a serious operation – a belief in a higher power can be intensely comforting in times of stress. For others, their prayers may come from religious communities or friends and family. Social media plays a very positive role in a situation like this.

Whenever I go to church, ever since I can remember, I always wonder why there are so many Black women in services – as opposed to Black men, who were just a small fraction of the congregation. Statistically, in the US Black women are the most likely to attend religious services and I'm almost certain this is the same within the UK too – just by mere observation, anyone would see this was true. Black women, in church, praying for our men, our children, praying for our families, then finally praying for ourselves. Our place of worship can also feel like the place where we release all of our burdens and heaviness through prayer. However, I am noticing that younger Black women within the faith tend to deviate from their elders in the belief that health services can also play a role in us accessing support. Ultimately, we can strike a compromise. Christianity and faith can be a source of strength – as they have been for me – but mental health services should also play their unique role.

The struggle comes down to this: some Black women feel pressure to perform extraordinary faith, seek help from church leaders, and 'pray away' mental illness, because they often don't think they have many other viable options. I had such a traumatic birth experience that it would have been unfathomable to confide in my doctor. My faith fills voids that are difficult to fill with other aspects of life, and the church fills in terms of community care, but we do need more.

The church is making strides

I believe the church wants to help. Religious leaders in the Black community play an important part in healing, and the wider congregation can offer great support to families struggling with mental health issues. But even in this welcoming and inclusive environment, it can be difficult for us Black women to get over the stigma, open up and look for the help we need. Black women, who are expected to be resilient, have trouble saying we need more than this. We need attention and care.

One female pastor I knew realized that there was a problem in her church and decided to start sessions for the Black women in her congregation to come and discuss their problems with her and others. She advertised these as 'Mental health, it affects us all'. To her surprise, even though she knew that many women in the congregation had issues, and as it was a young congregation, a lot of that was around perinatal mental health, only a couple of women came and those who did show up were very tight-lipped.

She thought about the problem and came up with a solution. She changed the name of the sessions to 'Our Emotional Health'. It did the trick! Her class was inundated with women. This confirmed the fact that any mention of mental health is likely to put people off and arguably that stigma still casts a long shadow. I am not naive enough to think that there is an easy answer to this – a magic wand that we can wave over it and just make it go away.

I think that there is no doubt that churches and religious leaders could do more to help take the stigma away from mental health and encourage Black women to seek the help we need. More could be done to encourage people into spaces in the church or place of worship where they feel safe to talk about the things that worry them. There is never any substitute for proper medical help, but by opening up in the first instance to a religious leader, it may be possible for a Black woman to find a route to the help that she needs.

I couldn't bring myself to think that God thought I was strong enough to endure another loss

It was the beginning of the week in mid-September last year and I had just confirmed a date for our first scan to see the baby. I think at this point the reality of everything had sunk in.

The end of the week was a completely different picture when my husband and I were getting ready to spend a weekend in London and after a visit to the toilet I noticed I had a mucus show.

My thoughts were:

Don't panic, you've seen this before and that baby is now a thriving one-year-old.

Do you really think God will bring you this far, only for you to lose this baby?

Maybe this is a sign that you need to rest, and not go to London.

So amongst all the other thoughts, the latter is the thought I acted on quickly. I put my feet up, but also called 111 just to be on the safe side.

A few hours later, after adhering to medical advice I was seen by a lovely Black female doctor who reassured me that she felt the spotting was due to the early stages of pregnancy and everything would be fine. Interestingly, she seemed more intrigued that this was a natural pregnancy considering my unexplained infertility diagnosis and history of assisted conception as well as losses.

After she highlighted how much of a miracle this baby was, this gave me more confidence that everything would be fine. She also kindly booked me in for a reassurance scan at the hospital the following morning.

I returned home that Friday evening and from this point onwards everything changed so quickly. The spotting had escalated to heavy bleeding, I began to experience bearable but unusual back pain, and so at this point the scan the following morning couldn't come round any quicker. Although the situation started to look less positive, once again I had encouraged myself and genuinely believed that there was no way the outcome of this would be negative. Whether this was down to faith or denial, and I presume more of the former, I couldn't bring myself to think that God thought I was strong enough to endure another loss.

My resounding thoughts were: I didn't even plan for this baby and you blessed me with a natural pregnancy so there's no way it would make sense for us to lose this pregnancy.

The following morning I woke up faith-fuelled and began to

get dressed for the scan. There was no way I was expecting bad news and so just out of excitement to see our baby, I took my first bump picture. I definitely now understand what people mean when they say you show much earlier on your second, third, etc. pregnancy.

We were called into the scan room soon after we arrived and we were met with the longest five minutes of my life. The room was silent and the sonographer's screen of fate was turned away from my husband and me. This was the very moment that I could actually testify and say I heard a pin drop. The silence in the room was so eerie, and all I could do was look at my husband's face with that 'grin and bear' reassurance smile that all was OK even though I knew it was possibly not so positive news.

The three things I remember at this point were:

- incorrect dates
- possible miscarriage
- ectopic pregnancy.

I was sent away with the curiosity of wanting to know what the blood test results were to confirm either of the eventualities above.

Many hours later the same day, I returned to the hospital at the emergency unit in excruciating pain, to the point that I had to be wheeled into the gynaecology unit. I was prodded and poked and further tests were carried out to ascertain what was going on. If an IVF cycle made you feel like a pin cushion, this experience far exceeded that.

A few hours later, after a late-night scan, I just remember the nurse saying to me: 'I'm really sorry but you won't be going home tonight, you need emergency surgery as soon as possible. Your baby is in the wrong place and you have internal bleeding. In the last 32 years I've worked here I have seen hundreds of cases like yours and I'm 98% sure this is an ectopic pregnancy.'

Whilst I tried to make sense of everything in my mind, I suddenly thought:

God how did it get to this...?

– *Vanessa Haye*

CHAPTER 6

Social Support or Social Smothering?

Culture and Community

I sat there in the dark bedroom with a baby in my arms and a toddler clinging to my leg. Tears running down my face. I was exhausted, I was tired on my own managing small children. Having to pour on to them when I myself was empty. Baby on my breast and toddler on my lap. They need me but I needed rest. I picked up my phone and dialled my husband. I couldn't do this. I couldn't cope. I needed help. Running a business, being a wife and being a mother. My mind couldn't cope. Something needed to give. As my husband answered the phone, I told him, 'This is too much, I have to give something up that I'm doing. I have to stop work.' I didn't have the support I needed, so I needed to navigate how to support myself.

Whenever anyone who is planning to have kids asks me about childcare, I say, plan as though you will get no support but accept it and lap it all up as you do it.

Raising children is not something you can do on your own. It takes a community. It takes a family, it takes friends. A support group is needed; don't isolate yourself. Make the changes you need to make to ensure your cup is filled.

– *Feyi Natalie Eshin*

I walked into the Mummy and Baby support group near my home, my tiny daughter strapped to my chest, nappy bag in my hand. *Please help me*, I thought. Surely these mothers would understand my struggle. The long nights, painful loneliness, lack of support from services, aching fear that I'd never feel like my old self again. I needed support and wasn't receiving it.

My own friends, as much as I loved them, were little or no help at the time. Most, if not all of them had not birthed children yet. Many of them didn't even have nieces and nephews. They didn't understand the stress of caring for a new baby. 'Sandra, you have a husband,' they all said. 'What more could you want?'

Yes, my partner was wonderful, but he was just one man. A man with a job and his own life, and sometimes it seemed to me as if he was coping with fatherhood a lot more easily than I was coping with motherhood. We've had conversations, and now I realize that wasn't necessarily true.

At the time, I needed help with things like cooking, laundry and taking care of myself and my newborn daughter. My hair was in a mess, and I hadn't worn a nice dress in ages. Where was Sandra fading to? Maybe I wasn't a woman in danger of falling below the poverty line, but didn't I deserve attention, care? Where were the aunties, grandmothers, friends? Where was my community?

My eyes darted around the room, studying face after face. *Oh dear*, I thought, heart sinking. *They're all white women. Where the heck are the Black mothers?* I'd heard that Black women were the least likely to access services, but this was ridiculous. My health visitor, an older white woman herself, had handed me a flyer for this very support group. Was this the type of help that she honestly thought would be of benefit to me?

Don't be so quick to judge people, Sandra, I told myself. Maybe these mothers and I would get along well. Maybe my new best friend was sitting just a few feet away. *Maybe...*

Very quickly, my worst fears were realized. None of the women were interested in talking to me about anything more than the weather, if that. They seemed to already have their own little cliques and circles. When it came time to change my daughter's nappy, I noticed – to my horror! – that I'd forgotten wipes.

'Excuse me,' I tapped one woman on the shoulder. 'Do you have any extra nappy wipes?'

'You didn't bring any?' she asked, eyes wide, creases on her forehead, frowning severely. 'I never leave the flat without them.' She pulled a container out of her bag and handed it to me.

'I forgot them,' I said in a small voice.

I hadn't thought it possible, but I felt worse here than I had been isolated alone in my own home. I imagined these new mothers looking down on me, mouthing in unison, *You're a bad mum.* I wanted to shout back, *I'm not! Look at my clean home! Look at my homemade meals. Look at how much effort I put into loving my daughter.*

I remembered my earlier encounter with social services at the hospital and pushed back tears. I couldn't slip up and forget nappy wipes. I had to be a perfect mum.

Nigerian support systems are legendary

Nigerian support systems are legendary. In Nigeria, when a mother gives birth, the whole village rises to the occasion. Elders rush in to teach new mothers about motherhood. 'Good mothers do *this*! Wait, don't do *that*, it's bad luck.' Aunties and other family members come over with food and drinks. Everybody celebrates. Workers, nannies and paid helpers move right in. My own cousins in Nigeria had one nanny *per child*. Each nanny has her own room! New mothers are never alone if they don't want to be. They have a whole network. This probably means they can get a little more sleep, warm meals and possibly time for themselves.

It's sad that I grew up expecting this level of support, but in the

UK women don't usually receive this type of care. Still, I imagined a world where my mother, aunties and mother-in-law all stepped in to make my life easier after birth. Why wouldn't they? In Nigeria, if the mother can't take care of another baby, her community intervenes. I remember listening to stories about the Igbo children my grandmother took in when their parents couldn't support them. She fed them plates full of Nkwobi, fufu, jollof rice without batting an eye. *Nni bu ndu*, she used to tell us. 'Food is life.' For Nigerians, babies are life, too. A child is an undisputed blessing for the family and community.

By the time I got pregnant, my mother had moved back to Nigeria. My beloved aunt had passed away years before. Another aunty was based in the States, and a third aunty was still in Nigeria. Who was going to help me? Where was the community of strong Igbo women I'd been promised?

I was blessed that my mother-in-law came to stay with us after my first daughter was born, though her support didn't come without a cost.

Omugwo is the Igbo term for traditional postpartum care. A mother, mother-in-law or close female relative comes to care for the new mother and baby. They take on most of the household chores. This includes keeping the baby at night so mum can catch up on sleep, but also preparing spicy pepper soup, hot water massages to help loosen and flush out clots after delivery, and showing new mothers how to bind their stomachs.

'This hurts,' I told my mother-in-law when she tried to bind my stomach. 'To be honest, it's not really my priority to have a snatched waist right now.'

'You're going to regret it. Talk to me in five years,' she said as she shook her head.

The mother or mother-in-law also prepares the ritual meal – *Ji mmiri okou* (Yam Pepper Soup with fish) and *Ofe Nsala* (White Soup) for the new mother. The meals are prepared with lots of sizzling spices. Igbo people believe that feeding the nursing mother lots of spicy meals enhances breast milk production and removes blood clots.

I was grateful that my mother-in-law wanted to help, but she had so many rules and traditions. In Nigeria, mothers receive a lot of attention, but they aren't the ultimate authority over their own children. Communal wisdom reigns supreme. 'You have to add bottle milk not just breastfeed, Sandra,' my mother-in-law insisted. 'Otherwise your baby will be weak and thin.'

As someone born in the UK, I was still used to being in control of my own life – for the most part. I valued highly what older women had to say, but I didn't always bend to traditional Igbo rules. Of course, I thought I knew what my own baby needed. When I questioned my mother-in-law, she made me feel spoiled, and then I felt criticized for disobeying our customs and traditions. 'You think you know best, Sandra,' she said, smiling. 'But you don't know better than generations of Igbo women.'

For all our rules, I did sometimes feel grateful to be Igbo. In Igbo land, the family usually shares the birth of the new baby by simply rubbing powder on their necks and then there's a dedication ceremony three months after the baby is born. That gave me at least 12 weeks to recuperate.

I knew that other Nigerian tribes had different customs after giving birth. For example, Yoruba families take naming ceremonies pretty seriously. So much thought, research, family tradition and history goes into picking a name in Yoruba culture. They plan a ceremony seven days after the birth. The ceremony begins with a small prayer and the introduction of the baby; the elder will then officiate the celebration with seven symbolic items that are traditionally used to express the hope or path of a successful life, and often he rubs the items on the child's lips. The items can be water, salt, honey and/or sugar, palm oil, kola nut, pepper, dried fish. Nowadays, this practice has the mum tasting the items on behalf of the child. Once the elder or pastor announces the baby's names, the party and food commence.

Yoruba women are encouraged to plan a huge party for the child's naming ceremony right after birth, which can be exciting for some new mums but overwhelming for others; dancing in celebration with stomachs out can be both beautiful and unbearable.

By the time my second daughter was born, I felt resigned to my fate. I'd come to accept that healthcare services weren't much help to me. Many women in my position are not aware of the services available to us. Others avoid them due to bad past experiences or assumptions that care would not be sensitive to our needs. I, for example, never really let go of the fear that someone might try to take my babies away.

While I thanked my mother-in-law for her African wisdom, her smothering care felt as much a burden as an asset. After ten months of her living with us – and me begging my husband to respectfully ask her to leave – I finally convinced her to go home, which was heartbreaking for both of us. So much for my community of strong Nigerian women.

I was able to find some support at my local church that I searched to find. I made it my mission to befriend the African aunties, though not all of them were Nigerian, and many came from different tribes. 'Sandra, it's us! We've got nappies!' they'd cheerfully call, knocking on my door in the afternoon. 'Here, give the baby to us. Go take a nap.' It wasn't the real thing, not what I'd dreamed of having, but it was definitely close enough.

I couldn't escape the feeling that my real needs would never be met. So why bother? One afternoon, I strapped my youngest daughter to my chest and put my older one in the pram. *Time to make spicy pepper soup for myself and my little ones*, I thought. *With or without help*. It was hot, and I felt tired, but I pushed along, my postpartum body still aching. I wandered up and down the market aisles when I felt a soft hand touch my shoulder.

'Hello, Sandra. How are you doing?'

It was the Nigerian aunty who'd sewn my traditional wedding dress. She looked splendid in her beautiful clothes and elegant shawl. I realized how beaten down I must look in my trainers, T-shirt with dried milk stains and oversized leggings.

'Hi, Aunty. I'm doing okay. How are you?'

'You know, it's not good for a mum to leave her house like this,' she said. 'Not with such tiny children. Where is your mother? She should be helping you in this market.'

I tried to smile. 'She's back in Nigeria.'

The aunty shook her head. 'What? No! She's supposed to be here with you.'

I wanted to cry. *Yes, she should be*, I thought. I missed my mum. Suddenly, the ingredients for the pepper soup I wanted to make didn't seem so appealing at this moment... I mourned the community I'd been promised as a child.

For better or worse, I've learnt to ask for a lot less. From friends, family and my community at large, but I'm saddled with the obligations of both worlds. I'm afraid of the cost of disappointing each.

When it comes to my friends, I understand I can't put enormous obligations and expectations on anyone who doesn't yet have children. They don't understand how much effort and stress it takes to function as a mum with little ones, so can they really empathize when they have not yet embarked on this life-changing journey? I was so desperate for contact as a new mum that two weeks after I gave birth to my first child I took a train to London to go for a meal with one of my best friends. My breasts were aching with milk, and I felt exhausted, but I was too lonely to refuse her invitation. 'I'm ready to dance,' I lied. *See? I'm the same old Sandra. Just as fun as before.* But what I *really* needed was for my friends to come over and hold my baby while I showered, rested and maybe even read a book.

Now that my kids are a bit older, there is light at the end of the tunnel – in fact, I honestly believe that I'm currently walking in the light out of the tunnel. I know more Black mums through The Motherhood Group, social media and day-to-day interactions. I have better boundaries with my mother-in-law, who comes to visit a few times a year. Some of my friends have started having their own children, and I see the same patterns repeating themselves.

Growing up in a single-parent household, where your mother has had to provide for four children by herself, will definitely influence your concept of independence. But whether you like it or not, once you become a single parent (or even a parent with your partner still by your side), you have to learn to have some level of dependence on those around you. You are mentally designed to only deal with so much; as resilient as we are, we still have limits, and it is okay to acknowledge those limits and ask for help.

Another thing I have come to learn is that as much as you are looking for ways for others to help you and establish your foundation, you too should look at the ways in which you can also help other parents. A bit of give and take goes a *long* way. You will begin to feel as though you are also of value and importance to those you consider near and dear by being there when you can.

Knowing that you too can help a parent in need will make it easier for when you are asking for help and support for yourself. It should hopefully help with that dreaded feeling of thinking you are becoming a burden unto someone (which, from what I have observed, a lot of Black mothers tend to feel when it comes to asking for help). And should hopefully be replaced with a feeling of doing good to receive good.

Remember, it takes a village, a community, to raise a child and you too are a part of this community. Every little helps and makes a difference to a parent, especially a single parent. Even if it is as small as picking up your child's friend from school, so that the parent does not have to rush from work and has time to do some grocery shopping on the way home instead, uninterrupted (it's the little things that count right?!).

– *Yvonne Ihegborow*

Black mothers have been said to have a reputation for being 'difficult to reach'. We're not. The NHS has trouble reaching us because they haven't had much history in asking us what we need. They also need to better understand our community, our cultural practices, our preferences and our expectations of what good support looks like – for us.

I honestly believe that if services work better together with the communities that many of us are embedded in, transformation of care can truly happen. Understanding our cultural practices means understanding us, and this should improve the quality of care and support provided for Black mothers as a whole.

Time, resources and energy should be invested in services establishing community-based relationships, while creating space for holding honest conversations about our cultural practices that make us feel more supported, confident and respected on our motherhood journey.

A dialogue between the services and women like me, split between two worlds, but ultimately individuals, needs to happen.

Understand me, Sanda Igwe, as a person.

Not just as a BAME mother.

Not just a Nigerian woman.

I grew up in London with a foot in Nigerian culture, but I have my own needs.

I struggled with postpartum depression.

I have obligations to my traditions that services didn't make an effort to understand.

My most valuable lesson 21 months into motherhood is that asking, receiving or needing help does not take any value away from me as a mother.

When I decided to keep my pregnancy, I viewed life as me and my baby versus the world.

I didn't go down the traditional road of dating, marriage and family planning.

My daughter's arrival in my womb was an unwanted surprise.

But something told me that I had to keep her.

And with this decision, she is entirely my responsibility.

I would take her to Leeds at two months old to deliver a university talk.

I would schedule Zoom calls to sync with her naps.

Eventually, however how much I juggled, I simply could not manage to raise Nyn and carry out my other duties.

So, I asked.

I asked the few friends that I have.

My foster family live two hours away in Bournemouth so I didn't ask them, and it was the Covid-19 pandemic with full-force lockdown.

I asked members of my biological family. Some declined. But some said yes.

One yes meant that I could attend a booking.

One yes meant I could have an hour to tidy our home.

One yes meant that I could enjoy a bath alone.

My biggest lesson in 21 months of motherhood is to ask for support.

Time away from your little one doesn't take away the fact that you are a super mum!

– *Yem Akingbade @thisisyem*

Black motherhood is strong, and attuned. Look out for and bring out the best in their children. Guided by the 4Is – insight, intuition, innovation, involvement. She engages, empower and establishes her children and many others that come/cross her path. She is always ready to go above and beyond!

– *Anonymous*

First thing that came to mind was family and friends. Also what support is available to Black women. As a young parent, I found my journey was a lot different from my social group. I'm sure older parents may have this in common, too. Living in mother and baby hostels really opened my eyes. Most of the girls there had little or no family support. Their friend was the key worker at the hostel. Me, on the other hand, I had quite a lot of support despite living in these circumstances. Twelve years on social support is still a significant part of life for everyone. We are learning every day and will continue to do so until it is our time to move on in life.

– *Anonymous*

I gave birth and should have been complete, but I was alone. Why? I felt clueless, had so much support but it felt pointless. 'It takes a village', so they say...but somehow my village wasn't village-ing. Everyone offered help but they had their own lives to live. So how do I get help when I need it? I cried and cried before asking for help...times where I needed to shower, I'd call for my friends to watch him so I could shower. The thing I taught myself was that looking after your child is looking after yourself. So now although I feel guilty, bad and all manner of emotions when I leave him to do things I need to do, I remember that I indirectly do it for him by doing it for me. So now I speak, I ask and do whatever it takes to do better for my family. I am a Black mother and I ask confidently for help.

– Christiana

There are many aspects to motherhood that although we imagine what we want from it, we know actually getting it is not a likely possibility. Things like full night's sleep, bounce-back bodies and body systems, babies that do exactly as you want and much more that you actually deluded yourself as a mother to believing could happen. These are the kind of situations we deem as 'wishful thinking'.

This village people speak of. While I was pregnant, I honestly thought with the amount of people in my life that love and care for me, raising this baby will be super easy... Wrong! Now, let me be very clear that this is not in any way to diss or throw shade at anyone, because actually the deluded person in this situation was me. This is a personal experience, so it could be very different for others, but I really thought I would have more people involved in my children's life than there actually are. The reality is that there are friends' names that my children don't even know, regardless of how good friends we are. The village was not as big as I thought. To be honest, the initial realization of this quite crushed me, but with time I came to understand that my expectations were not other people's obligations, so it's something I needed to check myself about and change my views on the types of relationships that my friends and children could realistically share. I purposely chose to share this as an example because it is not actually an obvious problem as a mum, but it was a real one for me and could be for someone else. It sounds so selfish to think that other people need to be deeply involved with raising your child or at least helping out, but in fact they don't and most likely won't. Of course, you do have that one or two that are involved constantly, but these are one of the things you need to be realistic about sooner rather than later.

There is the most obvious problem when it comes to Black mums and mental health – culture! Black women are raised on a 'suck it up' culture, so before you even become a mother, the thought that it could affect your mental health does not cross your mind. You can get prepared for anything and everything motherhood related, but what you are not spoken to about, warned about or discussed with is how it can affect your mental health. It's sad because when you have a baby, you literally enter into a new world and, without realizing, a lot of your old world fades away quite quickly. For that fact alone, finding a person to pour out to becomes much more difficult than it should be. Your own mum or mother figure – you would think that's the person to go to and, luckily, for most it is, but even when you think you're going to speak to them, that 'suck it up' mentality comes creeping right back in and immediately you're silenced before you even speak. This is how they were raised, so by default this is what you are made to think, so you do just that – you suck it up! You suck it up and in the process it sucks you up. You carry on 'as you should'; it comes with the role, so why should you complain? And before you know it, that's what you think you are doing: complaining. You are made to feel like you can't express your feelings because you are hit back with phrases like 'that's motherhood for you' or 'welcome to motherhood', but never 'that's okay, it's natural to feel like this and this is how you can deal with that'. So because we are often met with the first two responses, we just don't speak at all.

– *Tobi Oyedele*

'It takes a village' to raise a child

We all become mothers for distinct reasons, at various stages, with different circumstances and various strengths, but do any of these variables allow society to dictate our vulnerability?

Every mother at any stage will struggle or suffer for one reason or another. While everyone's personal struggle is valid, it is undeniable that some suffer more than others. I am a mother of four children. With every child that is born, a new mother was born in me. I have experienced traumatic birth, euphoric birth, and parental bonding with a child born from another woman's womb.

As a 'normal' mother, I cook, I clean, I support, I educate, I heal, I guide, I learn and grow, I make mistakes, I have bad days, I get angry, I swear, I drink wine, I love, and I laugh and everything in between. However, as a disabled Black woman, experiencing constant microaggressions, the perpetuation of stereotypes, and the continual invalidation of my experiences, it will come as no surprise I have also suffered with poor perinatal mental health in the past.

If you look at the animal kingdom, unlike us, their behaviour is instinctively led and generational. When a calf is born, it is surrounded by cattle. When a baby is born, they need not only their parents but their village too.

Pregnancy is a mother preparing for the marathon that is parenthood. We need our team to help train, guide and support us. Humans desperately need others as, unlike many mammals that within hours of being born are able to get up and walk, we can take months and even years to gain that same level of strength and confidence, which again we learn from those around us. Being forced into false independence is damaging and restrictive, we then come to see the repercussions manifesting in our behaviour and affecting our mental and physical health.

With my last child, I suffered from terrible antenatal depression, you know, the one we do not talk about. On paper, my life was great: my relationship, family and business were thriving. I had a great support network, my health was manageable, and we had just returned from a three-week all-inclusive family holiday in the Caribbean. Having had fertility treatment and multiple miscarriages in the past, this was my least problematic pregnancy despite being a complete surprise.

Yet I hit rock bottom so fast and so dramatically, none of us even saw it coming.

It was my husband and friends that got me the help I needed, who fought to get me out of my room and make me eat. Health services hardly acknowledged my feelings and asked me to self-refer. I had one psychologist that I struggled to gel with and a therapist that made me feel worthless and paranoid. I ended up discharging myself from their care and refused to take the medication prescribed. I found my way out through the support of my village and investing in my own education. This experience has led to me continuing to develop myself not only for me, but for the benefit of others.

Medication and clinical support have their place, but simply put, at that moment, what I was offered was not what I needed. I appreciate that I was incredibly lucky to find what I did need, and it pains me to think of where I would have been if I had relied solely on official channels to hear me and explore my needs. I may have been a different person today and still be unable to find my own coping mechanisms or set boundaries. In turn, this could mean that those dealing with perinatal mental health and birth trauma, to whom I now provide support, may not have felt safe enough to be seen and heard by me. This is cyclical.

We cannot talk about parenting without speaking about mental health because it is so deeply connected. Parenting is not one continuous experience, it is many, all overlapping and perfectly intertwined creating something beautiful and intriguing.

We cannot wait until mothers, birthing people and parents are suffering before we address it. It is like the rice burning in the pot and then throwing in more water. Why not top it up whilst cooking instead of waiting for the burn out?

It takes a village to raise a child and their parents. A new parent is born with every birth, and they need to be loved, nurtured, educated and supported. This support may not always look like family and friends. It could be a service offering the support you and your family need as you embark on your brand-new journey into parenthood.

– Leah Lewin

CHAPTER 7

Black Mum Joy

Listen and Reflect

When I set out to write this book, I knew it would be difficult to do my story justice without upholding certain stereotypes about Black motherhood. There are already countless stories about Black pain – especially Black women's pain – and it was never my intention to illustrate Black motherhood as one trauma after another. Birth, abuse, neglect, depression, repeat. Why would anyone want to become a Black mother if that was the whole truth?

While my transition into motherhood has not also been easy, it has been the source of some of my greatest joy. When I watch my husband throw our daughters up in the air and hear them squeal with delight, I do think at that moment that I'm the luckiest person in the world. I catch myself staring in awe at Zoe and Chloe, smiling – like, wow, I contributed to creating them? They love bangers and mash as much as jollof rice. They sit in front of the television to watch *Peppa Pig* in the mornings. They know the meaning of their Nigerian names: *God has written* and *My God will never fail.* They are a testament to my journey. They're happy, healthy and hopeful for their own futures. They remind me to have faith and to hold on. I make them laugh, and often they amaze me with their humour, too. Joy!

When I parent Zoe and Chloe, I try to give them the emotional care I desperately wanted as a child. 'Are you feeling okay?' I ask when one of the girls sulks. 'It's okay to be sad or angry.' I wish I'd had more healthy discussions around feelings growing up as a child, and I think if I had, I might have had an easier go of things in adulthood. I felt that emotions needed to be kept under lock and key. Emotions were a kind of weakness. And I never want Zoe and Chloe to think that their value is only in strength or their ability to repress their true feelings. Their value, and my value, is also in softness. In 2020, I wrote a children's book called *Zoe and Chloe's Feelings*[46] to show other Black parents that it's beneficial to start having healthy conversations with their children about emotions, but it starts with us.

My mother grew up in a different country, moved to the UK for better opportunities and did her absolute best with the tools at her disposal. She raised us by herself, and I know how hard she worked to keep us safe, fed and cared for. She was in survival mode and lost her mother at just 19 years old, without the expected support and community that she needed.

She had no choice but to be strong, which, of course, came with consequences.

Someday, I will have to sit down with Zoe and Chloe and speak to them about the realities of racism in the UK. I will have to explain how to deal with people who don't believe their pain, who don't trust their judgement or who try to touch their hair without asking. I hope I love them well enough to send them out into the world with the tools to keep them happy and safe.

No one is listening

I urge healthcare providers to start asking *how* they can help us. When Black mothers express our concerns, we aren't likely to be believed or taken seriously. What's the point of reaching out for help if we're met with indifference? We're so often expected to be superheroes, capable of solving all our own problems while also managing those of our family and community. I know now that I was less likely to get a PND diagnosis even if I'd found the confidence to speak with a health professional.

As I write this book, healthcare and mortality have been debated in the House of Commons. Politicians acknowledged that there was a lot to be done in maternity care for Black women.

Nadine Dorries, at the time the Minister for Patient Safety, Suicide Prevention and Mental Health, said:

> We are not afraid of setting targets... Setting targets in maternity units is what we are about, to make them safer places in which to give birth and to reduce both neonatal and maternal mortality rates, but we need to do the research on the near misses, to understand what the problems are... We are committed to reducing inequalities and to improving outcomes for black women – we work at that daily.[47]

We need to keep hearing these debates until they spark lasting change. There are so many problems, and Black mothers face deathly consequences when those in charge shirk responsibility. Our hospitals and clinics do not appear to be set up to help women with complex medical needs. Clinics are often based at different hospitals, meaning that women may have to travel to different appointments, and then when they do, communication between them is limited. Women are often expected to juggle other work and childcare commitments while attending many appointments. Not all women have the same support and security at home and at work, so it can be very difficult for some, and the system currently does not account for that. Taking all of these issues into consideration, how then can our healthcare services practically improve Black maternal mental health outcomes, when it seems that there needs to be a systemic change – a complete revamp? How can services be more responsive to Black mothers' needs with all the challenges I just listed when many structural and societal issues affect Black women's health?

The Motherhood Group was commissioned by NHS England and NHS Improvement to investigate Black mothers' experiences of accessing perinatal mental health services and the barriers they have encountered. Drawing on the analysis of the workshop discussions for which 191 mums registered, three themes were identified and explored. These include: personalized care; improving access to care; race and racism. Following these sessions, the Motherhood Group drew up the following recommendations:

Recommendation 1: Personalized perinatal mental health

1. Open conversations with mothers which focus on their health and well-being needs in the perinatal period from all health professionals in the perinatal pathway

   a. Improved conversations about a mother's wider support network and where they may be able to work with family, friends or community to support their mental health in the perinatal period
   b. Attentiveness to the concerns of mothers when speaking with NHS staff
   c. Avoiding commenting on the condition of the mother before addressing their concerns

2. Access and clear signposting to interpreters when needed

3. Access to perinatal mental health support outside of the mother's local area if requested

4. Permission for an elective partner to attend appointments if requested

   a. Greater support and signposting for partners to support a mother's perinatal mental health

Recommendation 2: Improving access to care

1. Provide clear information to all new mothers and partners during the perinatal period about the perinatal mental health support that is available

2. Engage with the wider community, including third sector organizations and peer support groups, to ensure women are given information about existing support networks (relating to breastfeeding, mental health, and motherhood more generally)

   a. Fund new and existing community support groups for new mothers, particularly those run by Black, Mixed, Asian or White Other ethnic minority women and mothers themselves
   b. Understand specific cultural factors which impact a mother's care or how they would like to access care
   c. Engage with service users and culturally specific third sector organizations to design services and promote community leadership roles

3. Ensure guidelines surrounding Covid-19 and health visiting are made clear to all new mothers and contact information for health visitors is easily attainable

4. Improved bias and antiracism training for NHS maternal health and perinatal mental health staff to identify existing assumptions about Black women

5. Invest in specific qualitative research surrounding Black, Mixed, Asian and White Other women's maternal mental health as a separate group, rather than employing the BAME terminology which many ethnic minorities do not associate with

   a. Explore the cultural diversity within particular ethnic groups (relating to: religion, family and kinship, neurodiversity, disability, gender identity, sexuality, socioeconomic position, education, etc.)

6. Improve and make clear the process for complaints in NHS maternity and perinatal mental health services

   a. Ensure Black, Mixed, Asian and White Other women are involved in leadership positions to ensure accountability and cultural diversity at all stages of service provision

Recommendation 3: Address cultural and racial barriers

1. Improved bias and antiracism training for NHS maternal health and perinatal mental health staff to identify existing assumptions about Black women

2. Review internal reporting systems and record who is being referred to social services by perinatal mental health practitioners

3. Promotion and recruitment of racially diverse staff within the NHS, including support for those training to become counsellors or therapists in perinatal mental health

a. Drive the development of a representative workforce at all levels, equipped with the skills and knowledge to advance mental health equalities

b. Recruitment of people with lived experience into peer support and lived experience leadership roles

4. Ensure a robust and accessible complaints procedure is in place for women who feel they have been discriminated against or treated unfairly due to their cultural, religious or racial background

5. Co-production of services with people from ethnic minority communities to ensure their specific needs are met

An understanding of racial disparity

The UK likes to pat itself on the back for a perceived lack of racism. Boris Johnson said that he believes Britain 'is not a racist country'. And although slavery is not the only way to oppress Black people, there does appear to be some sort of a shift. Tributes to slave traders and racist colonialist statues have been removed – which is a start. Many of my birth-related struggles – from the midwife who reported my husband to social services, to the nurse who refused to admit me into the hospital, to my less than satisfactory experience with Mummy and Baby support groups – can be and are traced back to racism. Unfortunately, unlike statues, healthcare services simply can't just be torn down or removed. Black mothers still need these institutions, just in a way that serves us and our community.

When I first went on television to share my story five years ago, viewers were shocked. Here in the UK? They didn't know that Black mothers were, at that time, four times more likely to die in childbirth than their white peers. They didn't know that Black mothers are less likely to be diagnosed with PND. The UK might not have the foundational sin of transatlantic slavery as part of its national narrative, but racism is alive and well.

One of the problems is that slavery is taught as the history of Black people and not the history of white people.[48]

Medical shortcomings

In general, Black women are more likely to suffer from mental health and healthcare inequality, partly due to incorrect medical assumptions about our pain tolerance. An article by Habiba Katsha, 'Giving birth while Black: Why is it so much more fraught with danger?'[49] covered the death of 24-year-old Nicole Thea and her unborn son. Katsha writes that the incident:

> shocked the country. Thea, a YouTube star, passed in mid July 2020, as a result of what her family believe to have been a heart attack (her autopsy is pending). She was weeks away from giving birth.
> While the exact circumstances surrounding this unspeakable reality are yet, unknown, it appears to thread into others. Namely, that Black women in the UK are four times more than likely to die in childbirth than their white counterparts; that Black pregnant women are eight times more likely to be admitted to hospital with COVID-19; that Black babies have a 121% increased risk of being stillborn and a 50% increased risk of dying within 28 days of birth compared with white babies. These issues affect Black women no matter how high up the poles of money and influence they climb.

While I was writing this book, someone asked, 'What if Black women had Black medical staff?' While that seems like a magic bullet in theory, I have siblings and close friends who are nurses. There are plenty of Black nurses in the NHS. Many Black women go into nursing for job security. Many of these women, at least from my experience, want to get out. They're afraid to speak about the injustice they see. 'I don't want anybody to think I'm a trouble-maker.' Most importantly, the decision-makers aren't Black. No number of Black nurses and medical staff can overturn medical racism without the full participation of those at the top with real power.

Ignored

I want to be listened to. So many problems in my birth and post-partum care could have been avoided if medical staff had taken me at my word and worked from the assumption that I was worthy of care. I don't want to always have to be a Strong Black Woman. I was then, as I am now, normal Sandra. I have emotions and fears. Sometimes I want to feel vulnerable. And I absolutely deserve to be taken seriously.

Even celebrities aren't immune from this treatment. I read the account of the tennis star Serena Williams, who went into hospital to have her baby.[50] She had a medical history of blood clots. While she was in the maternity ward, the day after giving birth, she began to feel very short of breath. She had had a pulmonary embolism before and was convinced that this was happening again. She tried to alert a nurse and to express her fears, but the nurse told her that she was probably feeling a bit confused due to the pain medication that she was being given. She continued to struggle for breath. She even told the nurse who was caring for her that she needed a CT scan and intravenous heparin. Serena was finally taken for a CT scan of her lungs, where doctors confirmed an embolism. Finally, she was given the IV heparin that she needed. This experience of being dismissed and not listened to, or the feeling of being an annoyance to midwives and other medical staff, is something I hear repeatedly.

Fear and misconceptions

Fear of speaking out can drive some women to despair. Kacie, a woman I heard speak, said she woke up every day convinced that she was not going to be able to look after her daughter. She felt she was not stable enough and admitted that sometimes when she took her for a walk near the cliffs where she lived, she wondered, *What if I just pushed the buggy off the cliffs?* I personally never felt this way, but can empathize with having such strong, inconsolable feelings. Of course, Kacie loved her child so much, but she was exhausted by the expectations of motherhood. Kacie thought she must be going crazy, but she was just suffering from postpartum depression, the same as I was. Every time she remembered her thoughts of pushing the buggy over the cliff, she would be almost paralysed with a sick feeling.

Kacie tried to distract herself by going for runs, but depression followed her wherever she went. She would not speak to anybody about it because she was afraid her daughter would be taken away. It was not until her daughter was almost three years old that Kacie finally got help in the form of therapy and began to understand what had been happening to her.

The fear that Kacie felt was not unwarranted either, as many more Black children than white are taken into foster care. It almost happened to me! Another misconception is that 'baby blues' is something that sets in immediately after the birth of a child, whereas, in fact, it can set in up to a year after the birth. There is also an element of cultural misunderstanding that comes into play around the diagnosis of the condition because doctors may not recognize how perinatal mood disorders manifest themselves in different ethnic groups.

Help – at a cost

When my mother-in-law came to visit after the births of both my daughters, I was grateful for her love and interest. I needed someone to help me with the practicalities of keeping the house clean, cooking dinners and changing nappies; I also appreciated the company, initially. As I've said before, in spite of her good intentions, her care came at a cost. When I didn't follow her instructions or partake in certain Igbo traditions, I often felt chastised. Having her around became almost as exhausting as doing all the care work myself. I wanted help *and* autonomy.

I think a lot of women feel this way. We want help from our families and health services, but we also want to feel that we can have an element of control in our own lives. We want to have the power to ask for help, and the power to say no. Yet when Black women approach our own communities for help, we're often met with shame. We lose respect. 'You can't do this yourself?' When we go outside our communities, we risk losing access to our children.

Maybe one of the first things that needs to be understood is that one size does not fit all, and that in a multicultural society, people need to be asked about their cultural and religious practices. This might well explain some of the tensions that prevent services from fully understanding Black women.

The problem of microaggressions

In addition to these factors, Black women also tolerate daily microaggressions that wear us down. Every Black person that I know, and this includes Black mothers, speaks of constant rudeness, microaggressions and stereotyping that often can derail daily life.

A week ago, when I was shopping with my daughters, a white woman reached out to touch my braids without asking – yet again. 'Stop that,' I said sternly, barely stifling a scream. The woman looked hurt, then offended. 'They just looked so beautiful...I'd never...', she stammered. Did she expect me to comfort her? Ignore it, like I usually do? After she'd touched me without my consent? *I'm not an animal,* I thought to myself. *You don't get to touch me just because you want to.* Small moments like these totally upset my whole day, make me less patient with my children and husband, and, frankly, hurt. A similar situation happened a few days earlier when a white mother that I do not know from anywhere touched my daughter's braids too – that time, I kept quiet. But quite frankly, I'm tired of letting moments like this slide. White people are more valuable customers than Black people. 'You don't belong here and you are inferior.'

I've often had encounters with well-intentioned white people who don't understand why and how their statements and actions towards me are offensive. That's the agonizing aspect of a microaggression: that a 'mild' insult and derogatory statement sends out a painful message to Black women like me. Even when it's unintentional, or appears borderline harmless, over time the microaggressions slowly drain us and ultimately negatively impact our mental health.

I remember at the start of the year my husband and I were speaking with a salesperson. As we started to talk, he asked me when I arrived in the UK. I smiled and politely told him that I was born here.

'No, where are you really from?'

I looked at my husband, and then proceeded to tell the salesperson where I grew up, a different part of London, and how we had moved to this new side of the area only three years ago. I could see from his facial expression I hadn't given him the answer he was looking for.

'Do you mean what is my ethnicity?' I asked. He nodded.

I then spoke about my family being of Igbo heritage but made it clear that my husband and I were born in the UK. I know he didn't mean any malice – he honestly seemed like a lovely man – but the ignorance of his assumption made me feel like I don't belong here. Constantly being reminded by white people that you 'don't belong' makes you internalize the pain of rejection and believe that there is something wrong with you.

One previous employer, like a darts player, threw microaggressions at me daily. It sucked the life out of me.

'Sandra, you are so articulate, I'm always so surprised!'

They would always find an opportunity to exclaim those words publicly in the office.

I had anxiety whenever I used a multisyllabic word, and I doubted myself when I delivered presentations – I started feeling as though the solution was to 'dumb' myself down, or play into the stereotype that they and many other people had of me. As the only Black woman in my entire team, I felt isolated, judged, and I felt like I couldn't just be myself.

Your mental health as a Black mother at work can decline even more. So many women I've spoken to have had to take time off work because of the constant microaggressions, along with discriminative biases, the frequent stress that it gives them, the migraines, insomnia and the secret tears in the toilet on their lunch breaks away from their baby.

Black women should be allowed to be themselves, fully.

Microaggressions are just as bad as overt racism, but harder to explain and prove.

Growing up Black – young Black women in the UK

Another factor to consider is the transition from Black girlhood to Black motherhood in the UK. The education system in the UK can often be the first traumatizing experience for many Black girls who grow up here. This can really scare people at a tender age if they're not lucky enough to hit upon the right support system.

If a Black girl in a UK school shows herself to be very confident and bold, teachers and school staff sometimes treat her with disdain and see her as a threat. Black students are punished unfairly for their *kissing teeth* or wearing certain hairstyles. I remember not being allowed on our school trip because my teacher caught me kissing my teeth (I might add it was extremely quiet, almost under my breath). As soon as I'd done it, she said I was being racist. To her. A white teacher. There was no dialogue about what kissing teeth even meant; she didn't know that's what I and many other Black girls did when we were frustrated and upset. She was immediately offended by me expressing myself as a Black person and she used her power to stop me from going on a school trip that I had been looking forward to. Instead, I stayed behind at school and had to write lines. I was a smart and friendly student, but she just couldn't see past my skin colour and gaslit me to believe *I* was racist.

Even if a Black girl has a very good academic record, it will only take one incident to eradicate all the success she has worked for.

From my own experience, I know that emotional Black girls are often written off for being *too much*. I earned great grades all the way from school through university, but my teachers often rebuked me for not paying attention, daydreaming and being a chatty young girl. I had undiagnosed ADHD, but the constant microaggressions didn't help. 'Sandra, keep your voice down,' teachers would say. When I went to the hospital to give birth, these original traumas re-emerged. Why do I have to fit someone else's idea of a perfect Black girl or woman to get respect?

Silence

I spoke before about the delay for Black women in labour obtaining pain relief. This is not always the case, of course, but when pain relief is denied, it can be a terrifying experience for the mother.

Without the normal reassurances of the midwives and timely pain relief, what should be a joyful experience can end up being one that leaves permanent scars. If a baby is lost, stillborn, Black women often shoulder feelings of failure and then disappointment of the rest of the family. Meanwhile, these same Black women may receive little or no support from professional services.

Motherhood can be a beautiful yet daunting experience, and that's okay to admit and say. Women need to feel confident in speaking their needs. Silence hurts us and our children. It puts us both in danger. I like the idea of healthcare professionals working with their community to create more comfortable environments for mothers-to-be to express fears and joy. At the same time, I believe all professionals should be educated on how to better support Black mothers and pregnant people.

Change

I'm grateful that so many have taken an interest in Black maternal health. When I give talks, run workshops and share my story, I'm often asked for further recommendations and resources. Indeed, it is important to want to understand Black women and our experiences; equally, it is not our job to teach white people how to humanize Black women and to have empathy for us. I'm not entirely thrilled that many of us Black women feel we have to showcase our pain to create change, but I understand this is often how history works. How change happens. Our silence has broken.

I also notice a change in how Black pain is talked about in policy and media, and while I'm grateful for the shift, I worry that our suffering is nothing more than the next media cycle. What happens when we stop making headlines? Will non-Black people still care about the plight of Black mothers?

Clinicians must understand our culture so that we get better and more informed care. A Black woman embarking on the journey of motherhood needs to feel empowered and needs reassurance and validation. For this we need to look at our own family and cultural influences, so that we do not pass on the Strong Black Woman mantle to our daughters. Of course, there are times where being strong and resilient literally can save us, but it is not beneficial to take the weight of the world on our shoulders and be responsible for everything and everyone. We need to dispel the myth that mental illness makes us weak or less of a person and overcome the stigma that is attached to it.

I encourage us to speak on our experiences, both negative and positive. And let us not normalize being treated as 'other', and although it is not our responsibility to end systemic racism, let us find the voice within to call it out when we feel we are subjected to discrimination. Targets will need to be set to prioritize Black women, and milestones achieved to lower the disparities that currently exist.

Black mum joy

Swirling, moving, dancing,
I've found my joy again!
Swaying, twirling, leaping,
A light at the end of my pain.
Relieved, this mum can breathe,
I was finally believed,
By my community.
It was they who fully understood me.
Although aggrieved,
By harmful preconceived thoughts,
Of who I should be.
No longer did I feel alone,
Silence, removed.

*My wellbeing improved,
I've found my joy again.*

– Sandra Igwe

It's hard to believe how many people I fooled, cheesy smiles all over my social media channels.

'My bundle of joy.'

That was the first caption I wrote under the picture of my newborn daughter. I posted it on Instagram, and I watched as my phone flooded with hundreds of likes, jubilant comments and what seemed like never-ending 'congratulations!' It was a confusing time for me, because I honestly had moments of happiness and disbelief that I actually gave birth to a beautiful baby – she was my bundle of joy – but I couldn't ignore my sadness.

My bundle of joy came with bundles of harsh anxiety, awful loneliness, gloomy dark nights, intense rage, mood swings and loss of appetite in my favourite meals. Yet I had no choice but to appear to ride the euphoric wave of artificial bliss.

Desperate, I wanted real joy. The joy that would allow me to share my truth, the joy that would allow me to own every single emotion, without shame or fear. The joy that would allow me to heal.

The first time I opened up and talked to another new Black mum about similar challenges we were going through I felt a rush of triumph. Like I had taken my biggest boots, and smashed depression in the face. And the more I spoke to other Black mothers, the more empowered I felt. The humiliation that once gripped me by the neck started to loosen, because I wasn't alone. They understood me. Although I never received a formal diagnosis for my postnatal depression, I knew that's what I had experienced, and I became addicted to the feeling of triumph every time I shared my story.

I know some people didn't agree with me speaking up about my depression. I was expected to keep the shame and stigma to myself – appear perfect. But my recovery started with me speaking up: about mental health, about the stigma within certain communities, about the racism that I have endured and about the system that perpetuates harmful inequalities that Black women face daily, not just within healthcare.

Becoming a mother and writing this book has also given me a chance to re-parent myself, to allow my inner child to come forward and say: *I deserve better.* To those of you who are not Black women, I invite you to use this book as a jumping-off point to investigate your own prejudices. It's not easy to think *I might be racist*, but it is the first step towards justice. To the Black women reading this book: know that you are heard and believed. Black maternal health is changing. Even if it's a little hope, I do have it, and I will keep working to ensure that what happened to me won't happen to my daughters and other Black women who are yet to embark on this parenting journey.

Notes

1 Emecheta, B. (2013) *The Joys of Motherhood* (2nd revised edn). New York, NY: George Braziller.

2 Kozhimannil, K.B., Trinacty, C.M., Busch, A.B., Huskamp, H.A. and Adams, A.S. (2011) 'Racial and ethnic disparities in postpartum depression care among low-income children.' *Psychiatric Services 62*, 6, 619–625; Watson, H., Harrop, D., Walton, E., Young, A. and Soltani, H. (2019) 'A systematic review of ethnic minority women's experiences of perinatal mental health conditions and services in Europe.' *PLOS ONE.* doi:10.1371/journal.pone.0210587; Amoah, E. (2021) 'Black, Asian and minority ethnic women and access to perinatal mental health services.' Maternal Mental Health Alliance. Accessed on 8/11/2021 at https://maternalmentalhealthalliance.org/news/black-asian-minority-ethnic-women-access-perinatal-mental-health-services; Morris, N. (2021) 'Black and Asian mothers face "deep inequalities" in postnatal mental health care.' *Metro*, 14 September. Accessed on 8/11/2021 at https://metro.co.uk/2021/09/14/black-women-face-deep-inequalities-in-postnatal-mental-healthcare-15254922

3 MBRRACE-UK (2019) 'Saving Lives, Improving Mothers' Care 2019: Lay Summary.' Accessed on 8/11/2021 at www.npeu.ox.ac.uk/assets/downloads/mbrrace-uk/reports/MBRRACE-UK%20Maternal%20Report%202019%20-%20Lay%20Summary%20v1.0.pdf; MBRRACE-UK (2020) 'Saving Lives, Improving Mothers' Care 2020: Lay Summary.' Accessed on 8/11/2021 at www.npeu.ox.ac.

uk/assets/downloads/mbrrace-uk/reports/maternal-report-2020/
MBRRACE-UK_Maternal_Report_2020_-_Lay_Summary_v10.pdf

4   NHS (n.d.) 'Targeted and enhanced midwifery-led continuity of
carer.' Accessed on 13/10/2021 at www.england.nhs.uk/ltphimenu/
maternity/targeted-and-enhanced-midwifery-led-continuity-of-carer

5   NHS (2018) 'Overview – Postnatal depression.' Accessed on 8/11/2021
at www.nhs.uk/mental-health/conditions/post-natal-depression/
overview

6   Chapple, T. (2021) 'Are black women getting enough support for
mental health?' *BBC News*, 20 April. Accessed on 8/11/2021 at www.
bbc.co.uk/news/av/uk-56765171

7   Ipsos MORI (2020) 'Ipsos MORI Veracity Index 2020.' Accessed on
8/11/2021 at www.ipsos.com/ipsos-mori/en-uk/ipsos-mori-veracity-
index-2020-trust-in-professions

8   Hoffman, K.M., Trawalter, S., Axt, J.R. and Oliver, M.N. (2016)
'Racial bias in pain assessment and treatment recommendations,
and false beliefs about biological differences between blacks and
whites.' *PNAS 113*, 116, 4296–4301; Holpuch, A. (2016) 'Black
patients half as likely to receive pain medication as white patients,
study finds.' *The Guardian*, 11 August. Accessed on 8/11/2021 at
www.theguardian.com/science/2016/aug/10/black-patients-bias-
prescriptions-pain-management-medicine-opioids; Al-Hashimi, M.,
Scott, S., Griffin-Teall, N. and Thompson, J. (2014) 'Influence of
ethnicity on the perception and treatment of early post-operative
pain.' *British Journal of Pain*. Accessed on 14/2/2022 at https://doi.
org/10.1177%2F2049463714559254

9   Andrews, K. (2022) '"We were made to feel like outcasts": the
psychiatrist who blew the whistle on racism in British medicine.'
The Guardian, 13 January. Accessed on 14/2/2022 at https://www.
theguardian.com/society/2022/jan/13/we-were-made-to-feel-like-
outcasts-the-psychiatrist-who-blew-the-whistle-on-racism-in-british-
medicine

10 History (2020) 'Tuskegee Experiment: The infamous syphilis study.'
Accessed on 13/10/2021 at www.history.com/news/the-infamous-40-
year-tuskegee-study

11 Zhang, S. (2018) 'The surgeon who experimented on slaves.' *The
Atlantic*. Accessed on 13/10/2021 at www.theatlantic.com/health/
archive/2018/04/j-marion-sims/558248

12 Gomez, A.M., Fuentes, L. and Allina, A. (2014) 'Women or LARC

first?' Reproductive autonomy and the promotion of long-lasting reversible contraception methods.' *Perspectives on Sexual and Reproductive Health 46*, 3, 171–175. Accessed on 13/10/2021 at https://doi.org/10.1363/46e1614

13   Pasquale, S.A., Brandeis, V., Cruz, R.I., Kelly, S. and Sweeney, M. (1987) 'Norplant contraceptive implants: Rods versus capsules.' *Contraception 36*, 3, 305–316. Accessed on 8/11/2021 at https://doi.org/10.1016/0010-7824(87)90100-4

14   Sabin, J.A. (2020) 'How we fail black patients in pain.' Association of American Medical Colleges. Accessed on 8/11/2021 at www.aamc.org/news-insights/how-we-fail-black-patients-pain

15   Johnson, T.J., Weaver, M.D., Borrero, S., Davis, E.M. *et al.* (2013) 'Association of race and ethnicity with management of abdominal pain in the emergency department.' *Pediatrics 132*, 4, e851–e858. Accessed on 13/10/2021 at https://dx.doi.org/10.1542%2Fpeds.2012-3127; Koodun, S., Dudhia, R., Abifarin, B. and Greenhalgh, N. (2021) 'Racial and ethnic disparities in mental health care.' *The Pharmaceutical Journal 307*, 7954. Accessed on 14/2/2022 at https://pharmaceutical-journal.com/article/research/racial-and-ethnic-disparities-in-mental-health-care

16   House of Commons/House of Lords Joint Committee on Human Rights (2020) 'Black people, racism and human rights: Eleventh Report of Session 2019–21.' Accessed on 13/10/2021 at https://committees.parliament.uk/publications/3376/documents/32359/default/

17   Summers, H. (2021) 'Black women in the UK four times more likely to die in pregnancy or childbirth.' *The Guardian*, 15 January. Accessed on 13/10/2021 at www.theguardian.com/global-development/2021/jan/15/black-women-in-the-uk-four-times-more-likely-to-die-in-pregnancy-or-childbirth

18   Birkhäuer, J., Gaab, J., Kossowsky, J., Hasler, S. *et al.* (2017) 'Trust in the health care professional and health outcome: A meta-analysis.' *PLOS ONE 12*, 2, e0170988. Accessed on 8/11/2021 at https://dx.doi.org/10.1371%2Fjournal.pone.0170988

19   Jacobs, E.A., Rolle, I., Ferrans, C.E., Whitaker, E.E. and Warnecke, R.B. (2006) 'Understanding African Americans' views of the trustworthiness of physicians.' *J Gen Intern Med 21*, 6, 642–647.

20   Psychology (n.d.) 'Patient adherence.' Accessed on 8/11/2021 at http://psychology.iresearchnet.com/health-psychology-research/patient-adherence

21 Huerto, R. (2020) 'Minority patients benefit from having minority doctors, but that's a hard match to make.' M Health Lab. Accessed on 8/11/2021 at https://labblog.uofmhealth.org/rounds/minority-patients-benefit-from-having-minority-doctors-but-thats-a-hard-match-to-make-0

22 Lakhami, N. (2020) 'Black babies more likely to survive when cared for by black doctors – US study.' *The Guardian*, 17 August. Accessed on 8/11/2021 at www.theguardian.com/world/2020/aug/17/black-babies-survival-black-doctors-study

23 University of Miami (2020) 'Having a doctor who shares the same race may ease patient's angst.' *ScienceDaily*, 24 August. Accessed on 8/11/2021 at www.sciencedaily.com/releases/2020/08/200824144315.htm

24 Kline, R. (2014) 'The "snowy white peaks" of the NHS: A survey of discrimination in governance and leadership and the potential impact on patient care in London and England.' Middlesex University London. Accessed on 13/10/2021 at www.mdx.ac.uk/__data/assets/pdf_file/0015/50190/The-snowy-white-peaks-of-the-NHS.pdf.pdf

25 Gooden, M. (2017) 'As a black woman you have to work twice as hard to get to where you want to be.' NHS Leadership Academy. Accessed on 13/10/2021 at www.leadershipacademy.nhs.uk/black-woman-work-twice-hard-get-want

26 NHS England (2019) 'NHS staff experiencing discrimination at work.' Accessed on 13/10/2021 at www.ethnicity-facts-figures.service.gov.uk/workforce-and-business/nhs-staff-experience/nhs-staff-experiencing-discrimination-at-work/latest

27 NHS England (2019) *NHS Workforce Race Equality Standard: 2019 Data Analysis Report for NHS Trusts*. Accessed on 13/10/2021 at www.england.nhs.uk/wp-content/uploads/2020/01/wres-2019-data-report.pdf

28 BBC News (2021) 'Daunte Wright shooting: Officer "mistook gun for Taser".' Accessed on 13/10/2021 at www.bbc.co.uk/news/world-us-canada-56724798

29 Horne, C. '"Black Dog": Depression and how it works.' Better Help. Accessed on 13/10/2021 at www.betterhelp.com/advice/depression/understanding-the-metaphorical-black-dog-depression-and-how-it-works

30 Hoffman, K.M., Trawalter, S., Axt, J.R. and Oliver, M.N. (2016) 'Racial bias in pain assessment and treatment recommendations, and false

beliefs about biological differences between blacks and whites.' *PNAS* *113*, 116, 4296–4301; Sabin, J.A. (2020) 'How we fail black patients in pain.' Association of American Medical Colleges. Accessed on 8/11/2021 at www.aamc.org/news-insights/how-we-fail-black-patients-pain; Bignall, T., Jeraj, S., Helsby, E. and Butt, J. (2019) 'Racial disparities in mental health: Literature and evidence review.' VCSE Health and Wellbeing Alliance and Race Equality Foundation. Accessed on 14/2/2022 at https://raceequalityfoundation.org.uk/wp-content/uploads/2020/03/mental-health-report-v5-2.pdf

31 Mararike, S. (2021) 'Mental Health: People from ethnically diverse backgrounds say help doesn't always feel accessible.' *Sky News*, 21 December. Accessed on 14/2/2022 at https://news.sky.com/story/mental-health-people-from-bame-backgrounds-say-help-doesnt-always-feel-accessible-12500754#:~:text=Statistics%20show%20BAME%20individuals%20make,to%2014%25%20of%20the%20population

32 Khan, L. (2018) 'Falling through the gaps: Perinatal mental health and general practice.' Centre for Mental Health. Accessed on 13/10/2021 at www.centreformentalhealth.org.uk/sites/default/files/2018-09/falling.pdf

33 *The Lancet* (Editorial) (2021) 'Miscarriage: Worldwide reform of care is needed.' *The Lancet 397*, 10285, P1597. Accessed on 13/10/2021 at www.thelancet.com/journals/lancet/article/PIIS0140-6736(21)00954-5/fulltext

34 Brown, J.S.L., Casey, S.J., Bishop, A.J., Prytys, M., Whittinger, N. and Weinman, J. (2010) 'How Black African and white British women perceive depression and help-seeking: A pilot vignette study.' *International Journal of Social Psychiatry 57*, 4, 362–374. Accessed on 13/10/2021 at https://doi.org/10.1177%2F0020764009357400

35 Bignall, T., Jeraj, S., Helsby, E. and Butt, J. (2020) 'Racial disparities in mental health: Literature and evidence review.' Accessed on 8/11/2021 at https://raceequalityfoundation.org.uk/wp-content/uploads/2020/03/mental-health-report-v5-2.pdf; Prajapati, R. and Liebling, H. (2021) 'Accessing mental health services: A systematic review and meta-ethnography of the experiences of South Asian service users in the UK.' *Journal of Racial and Ethnic Health Disparities*. Accessed on 8/11/2021 at https://doi.org/10.1007/s40615-021-00993-x

36 zandashé l'orelia brown (@zandashe) (2021) 'I dream of never being called resilient again in my life. I'm exhausted by strength. I want

support. I want softness...' Twitter. 19 May. Accessed on 13/10/2021 at https://twitter.com/zandashe/status/1394805726825099279?lang=en

37 Khan, L. (2018) 'Falling through the gaps: Perinatal mental health and general practice.' Centre for Mental Health. Accessed on 13/10/2021 at www.centreformentalhealth.org.uk/sites/default/files/2018-09/falling.pdf

38 Rogers, A. (2016) 'How are black majority churches growing in the UK? A London Borough case study.' London School of Economics. Accessed on 14/2/2022 at https://blogs.lse.ac.uk/religionglobalsociety/2016/12/how-are-black-majority-churches-growing-in-the-uk-a-london-borough-case-study

39 NHS England (2016) 'Specialised Perinatal Mental Health Services (In-Patient Mother and Baby Units and Linked Outreach Teams).' *Publications Gateway Reference 06050*. Accessed on 14/2/2022 at https://www.england.nhs.uk/wp-content/uploads/2016/12/c06-spec-peri-mh.pdf

40 NHS England (2016) 'Specialised perinatal mental health services.' Accessed on 8/11/2021 at www.england.nhs.uk/wp-content/uploads/2016/12/c06-spec-peri-mh.pdf

41 Mental Health Foundation (2021) 'Mental health statistics: The most common mental health problems.' Accessed on 13/10/2021 at www.mentalhealth.org.uk/statistics/mental-health-statistics-most-common-mental-health-problems

42 Cornah, D. (2006) 'The impact of spirituality on mental health: A review of the literature.' Mental Health Foundation. Accessed on 13/10/2021 at www.mentalhealth.org.uk/sites/default/files/impact-spirituality.pdf

43 Cornah, D. (2006) 'The impact of spirituality on mental health: A review of the literature.' Mental Health Foundation. Accessed on 13/10/2021 at www.mentalhealth.org.uk/sites/default/files/impact-spirituality.pdf

44 D'Acquisto, F. (2017) 'Affective immunology: where emotions and the immune response converge.' *Dialogues in Clinical Neuroscience 19*, 1, 9–19.

45 Cornah, D. (2006) 'The impact of spirituality on mental health: A review of the literature.' Mental Health Foundation. Accessed on 13/10/2021 at www.mentalhealth.org.uk/sites/default/files/impact-spirituality.pdf

46 Igwe, S. (2020) *Zoe and Chloe's Feelings*. Independently published.

47 De Cordova, M. (2021) 'Black mental healthcare and mortality: Nadine Dorries excerpts, Monday 19th April 2021.' Parallel Parliament. Accessed on 13/10/2021 at www.parallelparliament.co.uk/mp/nadine-dorries/debate/Commons/2021-04-19/debates/6935B9C7-6419-4E7B-A813-E852A4EE4F5C/BlackMaternalHealthcareAndMortality

48 B (@TweetsbyBilal) (2021) 'One of the problems is that slavery is taught as the history of Black people and not the history of white people.' Twitter. 6 October. Accessed on 13/10/2021 at https://twitter.com/TweetsByBilal/status/1445681197317689351

49 Katsha, H. (2021) 'Giving birth while Black: Why is it so much more fraught with danger?' Women's Health, 15 January. Accessed on 13/10/2021 at www.womenshealthmag.com/uk/health/a33323338/black-maternal-care

50 Lockhart, P.R. (2018) 'What Serena Williams's scary childbirth story says about medical treatment of black women.' Vox, 11 January. Accessed on 13/10/2021 at www.vox.com/identities/2018/1/11/16879984/serena-williams-childbirth-scare-black-women

Dear Zoe and Chloe,

Your entry into this world has taken me on a rollercoaster of a journey... Through the ups and downs, peaks and troughs, our love will eternally grow.

I'm hopeful about your future, but for now, I will speak up as loudly as I can so that you'll be heard, believed, supported and understood, in the way that you should.

Mummy loves you now, and forever xxx